# PRAISE FOR ENGAGEMENT

*"Getting associates fully engaged – their minds and their hearts – is what makes all the difference. This book provides straightforward, actionable tools to engage associates at all levels of your organization. Jack's A-Game is right here for you."*

MARK SKOGEN, CEO, FESTIVAL FOODS, GREEN BAY, WI

*"Engagement will change the way you think, act, make decisions and perform as the leader you were meant to be. Keep this book handy and refer to it often. It will serve you well on your path to becoming a great leader."*

MARK LEBLANC, CEO, SMALL BUSINESS SUCCESS AND AUTHOR OF *GROWING YOUR BUSINESS* AND *NEVER BE THE SAME*

*"Jack's long-term experience with CEOs is paying off with Engagement. Enjoy reading it as the guide to becoming a great leader."*

DAN WERTENBERG, VISTAGE INTERNATIONAL GROUP CHAIRMAN AND COPE AWARD WINNER

*"People don't wake up each morning to follow a theory. They wake up to be human beings. If you lead a company that has humans, this is the leadership book for you. This is the best leadership book I have read in years."*

DAVID HOULE, THE "CEO's FUTURIST" AND AUTHOR OF *ENTERING THE SHIFT AGE*

# EN GAGE MENT

## HOW GREAT LEADERS **IGNITE** A-GAME PERFORMANCE

## JACK ALTSCHULER

CEO and founder of Fully Alive Leadership

INDIE BOOKS
INTERNATIONAL

ISBN: 1-941870-17-1
ISBN 13: 978-1-941870-17-4
Library of Congress Control Number: 2015934179

Designed by Joni McPherson, mcphersongraphics.com

INDIE BOOKS INTERNATIONAL, LLC
2424 VISTA WAY, SUITE 316
OCEANSIDE, CA 92054
www.indiebooksintl.com

# TABLE OF CONTENTS

# DEDICATION

*This book is dedicated to my wife, Marilyn, and to our children, Amy and Scott. They are and always have been my reason.*

# What If...?

What if you could ...

1. Get more of what you want and less of what you don't want?

2. Live your fully empowered life—*all* of it?

3. Make a positive difference in the lives of others?

The first and third points are self-explanatory. But that second "what if"—well, that deserves a little explanation.

In the game of life, there are times when people–perhaps most people–sit in the stands watching it happen. It is "life as a spectator sport" and I don't recommend doing that.

I invite you to get onto the field of play for the entire game of your life. That is where everything takes place—life never happens anywhere else. *It is also where your greatest leadership effectiveness lies and where and how you can most powerfully influence others to deliver their full engagement — their greatest followership.*

This book is for you if . . .

- You have the simple yet powerful clarity to be a lifelong learner.

- You have found yourself in a position of leadership but your formal education somehow omitted guidance for success in that job.

- You believe you could get more of what you want and less of what you don't want, if only someone will hold a lantern to light the path.

This lantern is for you.

Jack Altschuler
Founder, Fully Alive Leadership
2015

*There are wide margins throughout* ENGAGEMENT *for your ease in making notes as you read, as well as lined note pages at the back of the book. Use page 163 to list the specific actions you will take to get more of what you want and less of what you don't want.*

**CHAPTER 1**

# Leadership Clarity from West Point

*"Leadership is the art of getting someone else to do something you want done because he wants to do it."*

GENERAL DWIGHT D. EISENHOWER
WORLD WAR II SUPREME ALLIED COMMANDER
WEST POINT, CLASS OF 1915

T he Hudson River Valley in upstate New York is stunning in its beauty. Its rolling and often steep hills are heavily wooded. Even with modern towns nearby with paved roads, beautiful houses, and satellite radio, the area retains a primal majesty of strong shoulders and of timelessness, hinting that Chingachgook, the last of the Mohicans, may be just around the next bend.

In this setting is found the United States Military Academy at West Point. Its spacious and stately grounds contrast dramatically to the thick forests all around, yet somehow the Academy seems to fit there.

Every autumn, a fresh group of 18-year-old high school graduates arrives to start their new path as West Point cadets. Each cadet comes with a notable pedigree, having excelled in high school academics and sports. They all bring glowing testimonials from people who declare the quality of their character, as well as letters of recommendation from their congressmen. These are, indeed, high-performing individuals, the cream of the crop.

These cadets will be pushed for four years to be the very best they can be, to excel in academics and sports and to learn things they didn't even know existed before becoming cadets. They arrive knowing they will receive a first-class college education, yet that is not the primary reason they are there.

West Point exists for exactly one purpose: To produce new leaders for the United States Army. That is why that first-class college education, as deeply important as it is, remains secondary for these cadets.

There is a tradition of leadership in the Army that traces itself all the way back to General George Washington. No army can succeed without great leadership, and understanding leadership is both scientific and artful. That is why great leadership is defined in so many different ways.

Many charts have been designed to help understand leadership and to clarify its difference from management. They tell us that leaders do "this" while managers do "that," all expressed in neat columns and starkly differentiated terminology. As well-meaning as the creators of such charts may be, they typically leave their readers with a sense of confusion and no clarity to help them on Monday morning.

The charge issued to the men and women who instruct cadets at West Point and who forge the Army's new leaders-to-be is to produce "Leaders of Character."[1] In pursuit of that they have done a much better job than most of defining what makes a great leader. Instead of multiple columns and lots of confusing terminology, they have boiled it down to just four words.

## BILL'S OFFICE

I learned about that in (let's call him) Bill's office one day as we met for his monthly coaching session. In my mind's eye, I can still see him explaining the performance of his sales team, about how they had responded so enthusiastically and successfully to his leadership. The starkly clear comment he made stunned me and became instantly memorable. I immediately raised my hands in a "time out" gesture and said, "Whoa. What did you just say?"

This West Point graduate said to me what he and the thousands of military academy students are told repeatedly. It is a fundamental law of leadership about which they are exquisitely clear at our military academies and it is a leadership mantra. I have adopted it as *Engagement Practice #1:*

## ENGAGEMENT Practice #1

# Manage Things; Lead People

These cadets are taught to manage things (policies, procedures, task performance, etc.) but to never manage people. The common term is "micromanage" and people don't like being micromanaged.

Yes, the United States Army has a long tradition of being authoritarian. Anecdotes depicting brainless leadership are legion. But that was then, and this is now.

The people who train our new generation of leaders for the Army have figured out that soldiers are human beings. They understand that micromanaging them is likely to produce both sub-optimal effort and sub-optimal results. That is why those being trained as new leaders for the United States Army are taught to manage things and to lead people.

The Army trains that way because that produces the best results—hard, pragmatic results created by drawing out the best people have to give.

If that authoritarian institution—the United States Army—has figured this out, surely others, including those in the business world can understand that, too.

## THE MANAGING PART

In my *Engagement* keynotes, I often ask for a volunteer, specifically someone who has been micromanaged at any time. Then I ask, "How did you like being micromanaged?" The response is usually "I HATED it!" Regardless of the specific words they choose, their responses are always laced with passion. That is because they felt controlled and manipulated, sometimes even humiliated, when they were micromanaged. Their sense of being in charge of themselves was assaulted daily and they were frustrated, even dispirited.

That is how we humans typically respond to being managed or micromanaged. Most of us extricate ourselves from that decidedly unpleasant situation as fast as we can. Those who don't move on often simply disengage and become poor performers.

Perhaps you were micromanaged at some time. If so, then you probably didn't care for it any more than my keynote and workshop attendees do. It is likely you "HATED it!" too. As a result, you didn't give your best effort to your tasks. That made things worse, both for you and for your leaders.

It is a simple extrapolation, then, that if you didn't like being micromanaged and if you responded with less than your best, it is highly likely that those who look to you for leadership will respond in a similar fashion if they are micromanaged. So if you want to get more of what you want and less of what you don't want, don't micromanage your people. Instead, be a great leader for them.

Noted researcher and author Daniel Pink, author of *Drive: The Surprising Truth About What Motivates Us*, tells us, "Traditional notions of management are great if you want compliance. But if you want engagement, self-direction works better."[2] Even more simply stated, Pink tells us, "Control leads to compliance; autonomy leads to engagement."[3] And no leader thinks effort limited to compliance is acceptable.

To be sure, the role of managing is critically important and, therefore, so is the role of managers. They create structure and, without that structure, we would have chaos. So, this is not meant to disparage managers or management. Rather, it is to clarify what goes where.

## THE LEADING PART

The second part of *Engagement* Practice #1 is to lead people. If you ever had a great leader in any venue of your life, it is a near-certainty that person did not micromanage you. You probably felt a special connection to that person, and had the sense that he or she saw you clearly and perhaps even cared about you. Furthermore, you undoubtedly loved being a follower of that great leader and you gave your best. You may have been inspired to do things you didn't even imagine you were capable of doing.

And so it is for those who look to you for leadership. Your success is directly tied to your people giving their best, their full engagement. And to get their engagement—their commitment— requires you to be a great leader for them.

Richard Hadden of Contented Cows Partners, LLC and coauthor of *Contented Cows Still Give Better Milk*, offers a most useful definition of leadership. He tells us that leadership is "The earned commitment of followers."[4] Nobody follows you and gives their commitment because you're a nice guy or because you're smart or good-looking. There are other very human reasons why people commit to you, and you have to earn their commitment every day. That is what great leaders do and that is what inspiring employee engagement is all about, because that is what produces the very best results.

To make the *Engagement* Practice #1 distinction a bit sharper, consider that most people like to be in control. Indeed, when we feel out of control, we humans become profoundly uncomfortable. Yet as Daniel Pink cautions, getting the best results, creating engagement, "…requires resisting the temptation to control people…"[5] So, the trick for you is to refrain from extending your wanting to be in control to attempting to control the people who look to you for leadership. That is because the more you try to control, the less influence you will have. Go ahead and underline that last sentence; it is that important.

Thus, the first Practice—and the continuing focus of *Engagement*—is to always Manage Things and to Lead People.

## CHAPTER 2

# Why You Should Care

*"You can't reach your full potential unless you help someone reach theirs."*

SEAN TUCKER
EAA YOUNG EAGLES CHAIRMAN AND AUTHOR,
*USING AVIATION TO PROFOUNDLY IMPACT YOUNG LIVES*

S tudies consistently show that you have much better results when those who look to you for leadership are fully engaged. That is why you should care.

For example, a study by the Corporate Executive Board (CEB)[6] showed that fully engaged employees are 87 percent less likely to leave, they try 57 percent harder and perform 20 percent better than employees who are engaged at an average level. Just one implication of the CEB's data is that if you could influence one of your people who is engaged at an average level to step it up and give his or her best, you would see a 20 percent increase in productivity at zero incremental labor cost.

Now imagine the dramatically improved results if your whole team became 20 percent more productive.

And the story gets better.

In a 2011 study[7] the Gallup Organization reported that if you could influence one of your people who does just enough to get by to shift to giving his or her best, you would see a *50 percent increase in productivity at zero incremental labor cost*!

Let's look at this in yet another way.

In 2009, Paul L. Marciano, Ph.D., president of Whiteboard, LLC, conducted a study[8] showing that when compared to companies in which employees were less than fully engaged (i.e., holding back their best effort), companies with engaged employees had:

- a 21 percent increase in productivity and performance

- a $0.39 EPS profitability edge

- turnover reduced by 75 percent

- reduction in employee fraud

- improved customer satisfaction and loyalty

- reduced defects

- improved safety compliance

- increased employee satisfaction

Data from study after study consistently shows that influencing your people to give their best is the most predictable way to ensure enterprise success.

Indeed, if success is what you want, your followers will have to give their best. Then both you and they will—

> *Get more of what you want*
> *and less of what you don't want.*

## MORE THAN A BUZZWORD

"Engagement" has become a buzzword in business; however, it deserves clarification because it is critical for success.

Employee engagement has nothing to do with people's skill sets or skill levels. It has everything to do with how much of their *discretionary effort* they are giving.

To understand what that means (and specifically what it means to you), look at The Discretionary Effort Continuum in Figure 1 below.

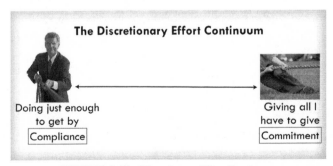

**FIGURE 1:** The Discretionary Effort Continuum

Everyone who looks to you for leadership falls somewhere on this continuum. On the left end are those who give just enough of their effort— just enough of themselves—to get by. They are threshold-level performers who are clearing the bar of performance only enough to collect a paycheck. All you get from them is compliance.

More than that, such disengaged people are often the complainers and sometimes the troublemakers. Their favorite activity at work is to enlist other employees in "ain't it awful" complaint sessions. They can be a direct obstacle to success.

In employee engagement studies, these people are described as "actively disengaged."

At the other end of The Discretionary Effort Continuum are those who give all they have to give—100 percent of their effort. These people give you their commitment and that is how all of the good stuff happens for them and for you. Employee engagement studies call these people "fully engaged."

There are two descriptors for employees who fall in the middle area of The Discretionary Effort Continuum: those to the left of center are called "disenchanted" and those to the right of center are described as "enrolled." It is easy to understand the effort and results you can expect from those whose engagement is described by these labels.

## YOUR INFLUENCE IS THE KEY

Be clear about this: Your job as the leader in creating success is to influence your people to shift to the right on The Discretionary Effort Continuum. The distinction lies in the word "influence."

Each employee makes an individual decision about how much discretionary effort he or she will give. Your part in that is to provide compelling influence so they make the decision to give their best. That means offering reasons for them to do so—and it is rarely about money. Indeed, it is often assumed that more money will produce improved effort and results, but that is not even close to the best you can do.

## SURVEY ON EMPLOYEE ENGAGEMENT

This issue of engagement is so important that the Towers Watson organization does an annual employee engagement survey. The researchers look at the state of engagement globally as well as from a country-based perspective.

Specifically, researchers examine both external and internal forces and the major drivers that create engagement. Reviewing several years of Towers reports provides a clear picture of how consistent the motivators for full engagement have been over time. This quote comes from the 2008 Towers report:

*The number one driver of employee engagement is the belief that senior [leadership] is sincerely interested in employee well being.*[9]

That is to say, the most powerful way to motivate those who look to you for leadership to give their best is to *let them know you care about them.* Perhaps such an intangible seems unlikely, but that is the biggest driver for your people to give their all.

Sadly, we aren't doing as good a job of that as we might wish. In their 2010 employee engagement survey, Towers reported:

*Just 38 percent [of workers] believe their leaders have a sincere interest in their well being.*[10]

Somehow, five out of eight workers are simply not getting the message that their boss cares about them. That is a problem, because it keeps them from giving their best and that assures less than the best results for everyone.

## CARING TOPS THE LIST

Yes, it is true that there are other motivators for engagement, such as doing meaningful work, working with people we like and respect, job security, appreciation, recognition, and more. But caring tops the list consistently. Indeed, caring is the heading under which most of these primary motivators may be found.

So if you want to focus on what will produce the best, most predictable improvement in the level of engagement of those you lead, demonstrate that you care. It is as simple and as deeply human as that.

Of course, you can just tell your people that you care. That might be nice, but it really doesn't stick. It may even be perceived as disingenuous.

In the final analysis, you have to show that you care and you have to do it every day. Fortunately, demonstrating that you care is simple, easy, and you already know how to do that. The purpose of this book and the *Engagement* keynotes and workshops is to serve as a powerful reminder for you to sharpen your focus and to make it all actionable.

## STYLE OR SUBSTANCE

Demonstrating caring is not necessarily about being warm, fuzzy and touchy-feely. Indeed, it could be about being tough and highly demanding. These adjectives simply describe style issues. Your personality and your circumstances will naturally dictate the way you go about your leadership and what is likely to be effective.

So, rather than paying attention to style, focus on substance. The people who look to you for leadership are always watching, so they get it—they experience the substance of your messages. Indeed, followers notice everything about their leaders.

Your people even know if your socks match.

Be clear about this: You lead by example, either intentionally or by accident. I strongly recommend intentional leadership, including the way you express caring.

This book provides guidance on critical leadership substance so that your people will get the right message and decide to step up their game. They will fully engage. And all you have to do is follow the Ten Fully Alive Leadership Engagement Practices:

1.  Manage Things; Lead people

2.  Ask Great Questions

3.  Listen

4.  Deal With Conflict

5.  Be Here Now

6.  Set The Bar High

7.  Deal With Reality

8.  Be Their Confident Captain

9.  Commit

10. Live All of Your Life

We addressed *Engagement* Practice #1 in the previous chapter. Now let's continue.

**CHAPTER 3**

# True North

C entral to getting more of what you want and less of what you don't want is clarity about what that means to you.

The origin of your definition lies in who you are, which begs the question, "What is a clear, concise statement about you that defines who you are?" That is to say, where or what is your "True North"?[11]

"True North" focuses on your authentic self. Absence of clarity about this can lead to crazy side trips from the road to success and even counterproductive activity. Worse, those crazy side trips confuse those who look to you for leadership and prevent them from being the best followers they can be.

To illustrate the concept of "True North" and how it works for you as a leader, here is my "True North" statement: *To be fully alive and to influence others to fully live their lives.*

That's it. I wake up with that fire in my belly every day. It is neither good nor bad; it just *is.* And I know there is a statement inside you that defines who *you* are.

## KICK OFF A NEW STRATEGIC GROWTH PROGRAM

Another illustration of "True North" comes from a CEO who invited me to facilitate a whole-company meeting called for the purpose of kicking off a new and ambitious growth strategy. Steve Isaf of Interra International, Inc.[12] had a plan to double the size of his company in five years. Naturally, this plan would become extremely challenging in the fourth and fifth years, plus it called on his already hard-working people to step it up even more. His immediate challenge was finding a way to enlist his people in his strategy, to motivate them to go to the plate and swing for the fences.

He started the strategy kick-off meeting by telling the story of the company, how he and his co-founders had started it at a metal table, sitting on folding metal chairs in a space he had borrowed from a friend. They had no company name, no lines of credit and hadn't a clue whether anyone would join them.

He told how over the years they had consistently outperformed their ambitious projections. His PowerPoint slides showed photos of his people and their accomplishments along the way. He had a little fun with his visuals by using seafaring images and terminology such as the course, the compass, the journey, the crew and next port of call. There was even some pirate lingo.

When he announced that the company would double in size within five years, an audible gasp filled the room. Everyone was working so hard already. What more would that ambitious goal demand of each of them? And why should they embrace such a challenging mission?

His employees might have guessed the CEO's reasons for wanting to double the size of the company were to create greater profit and greater opportunity. They might have imagined a bigger payday when Steve eventually cashed out. But he explained that it was for a very different reason.

With only the slightest pause, Steve said they were mounting this challenge for what he called "The Treasure." That is what he labeled his "True North" statement. It was to become *"A highly functioning team where everyone is achieving at their greatest potential."*

Nobody in the room except his wife and I had seen his treasure statement before that moment, not even his leadership team. So when he turned the meeting over to me, I asked all of his employees what they thought of it. Soon, a number of people were nodding their heads, so I picked one woman near the front of the room and asked what she was thinking. She said his treasure statement was "just who Steve is."

And that was the point. It was the reason for the plan—the "why" of it—and it was a reflection of "just who Steve is." Everyone in the room intrinsically knew that about Steve before he'd said it. However, explicitly conveying this reason to his followers had a profound impact you'll want to learn. More on that later.

## YOUR TRUE NORTH

Now, though, consider *your* answer to this question: "Where or what is your 'True North'?" Remember, it is not about platitudes, not about what sounds good, or what someone else said was important. It is, rather, a clear statement about what is true for *you*.

Go ahead. Put this book down and write what comes to mind as you contemplate this question. Don't worry about sounding good or smart or anything else. Abandon clever wordsmithing or crafting a perfect response, because perfect can be the enemy of the good. Instead, just focus on you and who you are at your core. Give it fifteen minutes and see what comes up. Go.

———

Was that easy? Was it difficult? If it was difficult, there are good reasons for that.

First, this is an unusual question for most people, and it requires time for pondering. Second, and more significant, your answer to the question resides in a part of your brain that does not have language, so even if you have a sense of your "True North," it can be difficult to articulate it.

Yet knowing your "True North" is so important that you must articulate it. You may have a vision statement on the wall of your corporate offices that is masterfully crafted and is mounted in an impressive and expensive frame. The people who look to you for leadership may be inspired by it. However, nobody follows you because of that vision statement. They follow you and respond as they do because of who you are. So the clearer you can be with them about your direction and priorities, the easier it will be for your people to align with them and with you. Your success hinges on that alignment.

## APPLY THE "FIVE WHYS" PROCESS

To make this exercise as useful to you as possible, consider applying the Toyota "Five Whys"[13] process. This was developed by Toyota's Executive Vice President Taiichi Ohno in the 1950s as a kaizen (continuous improvement) tool for root cause analysis (problem solving). This technique has proven to be quite useful in addressing a variety of issues beyond problem solving and has application for your "True North" clarity. Here is how it works.

Ohno discovered that if you ask and answer the question "Why?" up to five times, you will get to the heart of nearly any issue.

Take a moment now and apply that to the "True North" statement you just crafted. Ask, "Why is this important to me?" After giving that some thought, record your answer. Let that percolate for a while and then ask and answer "Why?" again. Continue until you sense in your gut that you have arrived at a clear statement about you at your core. And be patient with yourself as you do this; it may take a while to go through this process.

Next, approach someone who knows you well—perhaps a significant other or a lifelong friend. Tell this person you are creating a statement of "who you are at your core" and would like to get their feedback on what you've crafted. Then say what your "True North" is. If he or she replies that your statement seems really close, a little more effort is called for, so do the "Why?" exercise once more.

Then take your "True North" statement to your direct reports and explain its significance to you. Let them know this is the direction you are going. In fact, this is the direction you must go because this is who you are.

Let your followers respond however they will, but here is the key: *Telling them where you are going gives them a chance to align with you.* Your clarity will likely inspire your people and they will be happy to align with who you are and where you are going.

And your "True North" statement probably won't come as a surprise to them. Don't be shocked if they respond as Steve Isaf's employees did, with some version of, "Yeah, I knew that."

Your clarity about "True North" will be especially helpful during the hiring process for new employees because you will attract the right people, people who naturally align with your "True North." That will result in an organization staffed by people who all move in the same direction. And that is a key ingredient in the recipe for success.

## THE TREASURE

Steve Isaf revealed to his employees his "True North" statement—The Treasure—and as of the time of this writing they are embarking on the fifth year of their journey to double the size of the company in five years and they are right on track. He attributes a major portion of his success to his having provided consistent focus by telling everyone what was most important.

The reason—the "why" for all of their daily actions—was exactly as he had laid it out years earlier: *To be a highly functioning team where everyone is achieving at their greatest potential.* And that became the focus and reason for everything they do. Having that clarity has prevented crazy side trips from the road to success and has made decision making far easier for everyone.

Note that his treasure statement says nothing about profit or gross margins or any other metric. In truth, those things are outcomes of actions, not reasons for action.

Again, company vision statements may be inspirational, and that's a good thing, but people don't follow a leader and give their best because of that vision. They follow a leader because of who he or she is. By telling his people who he is and what is most important in such a clear way, Steve Isaf created the motivation for trust and gave his people the opportunity to align. Then, when it became time for action, his treasure statement was their "True North" that both directed and inspired their actions.

That is exactly how it will be for your people when you are that clear with them.

Here is a hint about the people who look to you for leadership: They want you to be their great leader. They want you to inspire them to be their best. Part of achieving that occurs by telling them who you are and where you are going, because in doing so you extend your trust in them and that will open the door for them to return their trust to you.

As a final note on this topic, I asked for and received permission from Steve Isaf to both tell his story and to identify him and his company, Interra International, Inc.

At the end of our correspondence he offered this:

*I have always said entrepreneurship is a spiritual journey. I don't mean getting down on your knees, although there are plenty of times you do that. I mean the fact that people believe in you and your vision and dedicate their lives to help you achieve it is very, very spiritual. You have a bond with them and you are blessed to have them in your life.*

*The question is what do you feel towards them? Do you want to create a place where they can achieve their highest potential? How do you reconcile that bond with company needs? Are you bound to have a conflict in the future?*

*I believe nothing is preordained and it is in the hand of each individual to determine the future and their place in it.*

# CHAPTER 4

. . . . . . . . . . . . . . . . . . . . . . . . . . . . . . . . . . . . . . . . . . . . . . . . . . . . . . . . . .

# When You Want Something Better

. . . . . . . . . . . . . . . . . . . . . . . . . . . . . . . . . . . . . . . . . . . . . . . . . . . . . . . . . .

*"You are perfectly positioned to get exactly the results you're getting right now."*

DAN WERTENBERG,
SPEAKER, CONSULTANT TO CEOs,
VISTAGE INTERNATIONAL GROUP CHAIRMAN

L ook at the epigram above from Dan Wertenberg. Do you think he's right? Of course he is. This is a corollary to the definition of insanity, often attributed to Albert Einstein: Continuing to do the same things and expecting different results.

If you want different results, you will have to do different things or do things in different ways. That is, you will have to *change*.

As difficult as it may be for you to change, the task becomes even more daunting when you have to get your people to change.

There has been quite a bit of research done on the subject of human resistance to change and there are significant reasons for this resistance.[14] Some of them are:

- There is comfort in the comfort zone and we human beings don't want to be uncomfortable.

- When there is change, we feel out of control, and we human beings much prefer feeling in control.

- It is hard work to learn new things and new ways. Many people simply don't want to put forth the effort.

These are significant impediments to change, but the most powerful reason for resisting change is fear of the unknown.

Knowing about the consequences of our actions breeds predictability and the comfort associated with that. Even if we don't like some of the consequences, we feel a sense of safety in knowing how things will work and what it means to us.

But when we depart from the known, we no longer have that certainty of consequences, and we become afraid. That fear is associated with a sense of existential threat that is as ancient as caveman times.

## CAVE DWELLERS

Imagine, for example, we are cave dwellers thousands of years ago. Every day, I exit the cave and turn left. Every day, I'm faced with the same scene, the same circumstances, the same challenges and opportunities. I know how the world works, and I have learned how to survive in my "turn left world."

Then one day, you grunt and gesture to me. You indicate that, upon exiting the cave, I should turn right. So I glance at the mouth of the cave, then back to you. I point to the right with a questioning look on my face and you nod. I respond with a caveman retort that can be interpreted as, "Are you kidding? I always turn left. Turning left works for me. Every day before turning left, I have this feeling of confidence that I will survive exiting the cave. Now you want me to turn right? There might be a large carnivore waiting there, hoping I'll become his breakfast. Needless to say, that scares me silly. Turn right? I don't think so."

Change always brings a dose of the unknown that makes us afraid. When that happens the highly advanced, logical frontal lobe of the brain is quite unable to deal with the flood of fear messages that come from the amygdala, the oldest part of the brain (often called the "reptile brain"). In that primitive area of our brains, all fear is existential. That is to say, fear is based on the imperative for survival and it has little connection to reason.

Put those pieces together and you have a powerful resistance to change—any change—as though it carries with it a threat to our survival. That is why people fear and resist change so powerfully.

## CHANGE IN THE FACE OF THE UNKNOWN

The world is changing, which means that both organizations and individuals will have to change. Indeed, Alvin Toffler, author of the landmark book *Future Shock*, is often quoted this way:

> *"Tomorrow's illiterate will not be the man who can't read; he will be the man who has not learned how to learn,"* which is to say, change.[15]

So, to be the greatest leader you can be and to influence your people to be the most engaged followers they can be, you must change first. Then you just might get your people to change—even in the face of their fear of the unknown. You cannot take their fear away; that is far beyond your power. But if you will learn, unlearn and relearn, you can offer them benefits—provide influence—that will cause their fear to be overcome.

To that end, Figure 2 outlines a three-step process to influence people to change:

## ENGAGEMENT

# Influencing People to Change

- Paint a compellingly attractive picture
- Have a plan and communicate it
- Mentor your people

**FIGURE 2:** Influencing People to Change

## STEP ONE: Paint a Compellingly Attractive Picture

Yes, you really do have to sell the change you want to occur. You have to show people how much better off they will be if they are to be motivated to change, not how much better off you or your company will be.

Consider that no rational human beings would change if they thought they would be worse off by changing. You have to convince them they will be far better off—so much better off that the benefits of change overcome their fear of it.

Let's look at this from one more angle. Think back to a time when you were a child and Mom or Dad said, "Because I said so." You probably did what you were told to do, but when faced with this kind of authority-based demand, did you give it your best effort?

Likely not. This imperative simply isn't compellingly attractive. In fact, if you want sub-optimal results, using a power play like, "Because I said so" is a very effective way to accomplish that.

The people who look to you for leadership need to know their "What's in it for me?" and it is your job to be sure they know. So, it comes down to this: In order for people to change and to give their best, the reasons for change must overcome their fear of change by being *compellingly attractive to them.*

## STEP TWO: HAVE A PLAN AND COMMUNICATE IT

People are smart and, while you may have convinced them they will be better off today by changing, they know that next week, next month, and next year are coming. They need to know they will be better off then, too—or else they'll likely revert to old behavior and practices.

When you provide people with information about the long-term consequences to them of change, it is reassuring to them and doing so provides a double benefit. First, they will probably both change and stay changed. Second, they will get the message you care enough about them to have thought ahead on their behalf. Because of that there is a good chance they will move to the right—toward greater engagement—on The Discretionary Effort Continuum. And they will do that just because they got the demonstrated message that you care.

## STEP THREE: Mentor Your People

If you want the people you lead to change, you will probably have to mentor them. This is of exceptional importance for so-called Millennials/Generation Ys/20-somethings. They are far more traditional than appearances sometimes suggest, and they especially want guidance in their professional careers. Indeed, one of the most important motivators for Millennials is getting continuous feedback about how they are doing.[16]

These people are called "digital natives" because the environment in which they grew up was digital, with almost nothing analog. They learned they could secure information instantly with the click of a computer mouse. That can result in them being uncomfortable waiting for feedback—that is, living with "not knowing."

In a business context, that means Millennials experience annual performance reviews as being 364 days late. That kind of delay leaves them without the feedback they need for either comfort or direction. It is an impediment to performing at their best.

It is likely true that giving continuous feedback isn't compatible with your schedule. Still, waiting a year for feedback doesn't work for your Millennials, so compromise. Have a conversation with them and negotiate a feedback schedule and protocol that works for both of you. They will get what they need to perform at their best, as well as the feeling that you care about them. Then they are likely to shift to the right on The Discretionary Effort Continuum.

And there is more to do than just giving feedback if they are to get the mentoring that is important to them. It may require a formal mentoring process.

If you are formally mentoring someone, keep in mind that the process is entirely about that person's development and improvement; it is not at all about you. Consider the following two guidelines for mentoring.

First, start by being completely focused on the person you are mentoring. Make it a closed-door, telephones-off, blank-computer-screen meeting. We human beings know when someone is fully with us and when they have half checked out and are thinking about something else, perhaps crafting their response to us or a pressing issue other than us. We don't react well to that (more on that in Chapter 6). If you want to have a high-value mentoring session, be fully present.

Second, direct the meeting by asking a focusing question such as "What is the most important thing we should be talking about?"[17] If you ask this question sincerely, you will likely get a meaningful answer that guides the conversation well. Responses will vary according to the person you are mentoring and by his/her current circumstances.

For example, the answer to your focusing question may be something like, "Let me tell you about my progress with the big project. I don't know where

I need to focus, so just be a sounding board for me and I'll figure it out." So, your job for that session will be exactly that—to be a sounding board—and to trust the person you are mentoring to find the most valuable focus along the way.

## DO PERSONAL ISSUES HAVE A PLACE AT WORK?

Alternatively, the person you're mentoring might be experiencing consequential and distracting issues outside of work. Maybe a child is sick or a parent has serious challenges.

In my *Engagement* programs, I ask attendees if a personal issue is a legitimate topic for a business mentoring session. Over the course of hundreds and hundreds of programs everyone has answered "yes." They tell me that if employees are greatly distracted by a personal challenge, they probably aren't being very productive. Chances are they're making mistakes and may be distracting everyone around them. Big personal problems affect the performance of people at work and can do so with enormous impact.

Engaging in a personal topic during a mentoring session will likely bring about two outcomes:

First, those you are mentoring may be able to let off enough steam to once again be productive;

Second, and far more important, they will get the message you care about them. Simply listening to what is deeply important to them accomplishes exactly that. As a result, they will engage more enthusiastically in their work and shift to the right on The Discretionary Effort Continuum because they want to do so.

Be clear that focusing on personal issues of those you mentor is solely about being real with people. It demonstrates you both trust them and care about them.

Be clear, too, that such a conversation is a one-way street: they talk and you listen. After all, you can't fix the personal issue for them. However, you can demonstrate your care by listening.

Actually, effective mentoring sessions fundamentally are about listening to what is of great importance to those you mentor, regardless of the topic or focus.

When your people bring their challenges to you your reaction may be to offer your solution to their problem. That is a natural human thing to do, as we are hardwired to be problem solving machines. Resist that reaction. Your job as leader is to bring out the wisdom and creativity of your followers. That means that in a mentoring session, the power is not in your smart answers; it is in your smart questions. More on that in Chapter 5.

If you are to become the greatest leader you can be, mentoring is one of the most powerful things you can do, so offer it to your direct reports. Start with an hour once a month. Then, with a little experimenting, you'll find the best meeting duration and frequency that works for both of you. Doing so will help your people to make necessary change.

And remember to start with that focusing question in order to steer the conversation to greatest value for the person you are mentoring. It is your job as the mentor to make that happen.

To recap Influencing People to Change:

1.  **Paint the compellingly attractive picture** to let them know how much better off they will be by changing.

2.  **Have a plan and communicate it** so they can see how their circumstances will continue to improve over the long term.

3.  **Mentor your people.** They want you to take an interest in their development and this is an exceptionally powerful way to do that.

Your future success in a world in which change continues to accelerate will depend upon your ability to influence your people to change. Using the *Engagement* Influencing People to Change guidelines will be a far more powerful motivation process for that and for influencing your people to give their best than by your saying, "Because I said so."

## CHAPTER 5

# The Power of Questions

*"The question is," said Alice, "whether you can make words mean so many different things."*

LEWIS CARROLL
*THROUGH THE LOOKING GLASS*

Were you the smartest boy or girl in class? Do you still hold that distinction? You just might. After all, you've achieved much—likely due in part to having really good answers to questions and really good solutions to problems, and your capabilities have carried you far. It is possible that being smart is how others see you, how you see yourself, and how you identify your self-worth. Being the smartest person in class can be powerful and compelling. But not always.

In my industrial water treatment company, I was the Answer Man. As Fred Rogers termed it in his children's television program *Mr. Rogers'*

*Neighborhood*, I was the Royal Smart Person. I was all ego-puffed as I dispensed my amazingly smart solutions and answers, and I loved that role. Right up until one of my key people told me I was an obstacle for everyone else in the company. He called me a bottleneck. I was stunned.

He explained that, because employees had to come to me for answers, action was delayed and that caused a lot of frustration. It also caused my people to feel as though their ideas were of little value and they felt disempowered. My being the smartest boy in class—the Royal Smart Person—came at a big cost.

We human beings are hardwired to solve problems. Throughout evolution, those who survived were those who were adept at this. Therefore, it is safe to say your ancestors were good at solving problems and their genetic encoding is part of your makeup.

If you are in a position of leadership, it is likely that people come to you for your experience and for your help with solutions to their problems. So, given your expert ideas and your evolutionary propensity for problem solving, you may be powerfully tempted to answer their questions. Yet, if you do that, your people just might have a bottleneck experience somewhat like my employees did; there is a price for supplying your wisdom for others' challenges.

When you solve problems for others with your smart answers you effectively tell them they don't need to think, because all the brainpower will come from you. But that leaves them dependent and discouraged. Doing this is also terribly limiting for your enterprise, as no one person is smart enough to have all the best answers all the time.

So to be the best leader you can be, to draw out the best your people have, their wisdom, their brilliance, and their creativity, don't answer their questions. Resist the strong impulse to solve the problems they put in front of you. Instead, do what great leaders do:

## ENGAGEMENT Practice #2

## Ask Great Questions

Here are a few examples:

- What are the options you're considering?
- What do you think is the best next step?
- Who have you consulted with, and what do they say? What do you think of that?
- Who else could you check with?
- How might you be impeding progress?
- Given the budget/time/scope limitations, how can you narrow your choices?

- What worked well for you the last time you faced something like this?

- If our positions were reversed, how would you advise me?

Ask questions like these and make up more, because it isn't about your brilliant ideas and answers. The entire point is to get others to discover their own solutions so that they bring their best. When you've consistently done that with your people, you'll no longer have to be the smartest boy or girl in class. You'll have an entire company of the smartest boys and girls.

## A RUSH OF ADRENALINE

In their article "The Neuroscience of Leadership," David Rock and Jeffrey Schwartz write, "When people solve a problem themselves, the brain releases a rush of neurotransmitters like adrenaline." That means we humans become excited, energized, and positive in our attitude when we solve our own problems. Likely, you've had that experience. Rock and Schwartz add, "This natural 'high' becomes positively associated with the change experience."[18] That means that when people solve their own problems, they find that change becomes easier both this time and the next.

So help your people do exactly that by consciously resisting the impulse to solve their problems.

Instead, *ask great questions.* That is what great leaders do to develop followers who are fully engaged.

## SILENCE

In American culture, we are uncomfortable with long silences. My unscientific research says that about twelve to fifteen seconds is the pain threshold, after which people become profoundly squirmy. That is an important point for you to know as you develop your greatest leadership and your next level of leaders.

When led by a great question, silence is a powerful tool for arriving at a more valuable discussion and better outcomes. In her book *Fierce Conversations*, Susan Scott says it this way, "Let silence do the heavy lifting."[19] Follow the logic on this and see what you think.

In your effort to develop the next generation of leaders, getting people to step up is critical. Yet those who look to you for leadership need a place to step into, and it isn't always clear where that space lies. In addition, many need an invitation into leadership.

So imagine being in your conference room with your direct reports, and you ask the key question. Then you sit back and simply wait to see who responds. Almost certainly someone will respond in less than fifteen seconds, and you will know, without it having been said, that he or she wants more responsibility—wants to step up in leadership.

Perhaps as important, you need to be aware that when someone responds to your invitation into leadership, that person knows there are consequences to failure. That is why your acknowledgment and appreciation is required in that moment. After all, he or she is stepping up for you because you asked. In return, show your appreciation for that. Your response might sound like this: "I know you're taking a chance, Bob. Thanks for stepping up."

## APPRECIATION AS MOTIVATOR

Yes, great leadership can be as simple as showing appreciation.

Surveys have consistently indicated that one of the most powerful extrinsic (what others do for us) human motivators is appreciation. If you are human, you already know how important that is.

Still, you can test that premise with this fill-in-the-blanks pop quiz:

> Mom said, "When someone does something nice for you, say _____ ____."

Did you answer "thank you"?

Easy clarity about this comes from James C. Hunter, author of *The Servant*, who said that being a great leader means "…meeting the legitimate needs, not wants, of those we lead."[20] Simple human appreciation is one of those needs.

Expressing appreciation shows that you care. It also invites others to step up the next time an opportunity reveals itself.

So, if you want your people to bring their best, ask great questions, let silence do the heavy lifting, and then simply say, "Thank you."

# CHAPTER 6

# Telling the Truth in All Ways

*"Twenty-first century leaders need to be better listeners."*

JEFF IMMELT, CEO
GENERAL ELECTRIC
*FORTUNE* MAGAZINE, MARCH 22, 2010

The 1986 motion picture *Hoosiers*[21] is more than a sports film. It is also more than the coming-of-age story that it appears to be. Viewed through the *Engagement* lens, it contains messages aplenty about what great leadership looks like (and sometimes what it does not look like) and the kind of engagement that great leadership engenders. Let's look at two important pieces from that story.

The movie is set in the fictional small town of Hickory, Indiana during high school year 1951-

1952. It was a time when basketball players wore short athletic shorts and cheerleaders wore long, heavy wool skirts. In every rural Indiana town in those days, high school sports were everything. The whole town turned out for each sporting event, making the job of coaching high school teams a high-pressure occupation.

In the movie, the team from Hickory has an excellent basketball season. Then they win in post-season play, making it to the state championship tournament in Indianapolis. They continue winning until at last they're playing in the final game for the state championship, facing the powerhouse team from South Bend Central High School.

In the climactic scene, only nineteen seconds remain in the game, the score is tied at 40 and the team from Hickory has just called a time out to huddle with the coach. They only have that thirty-second time out to decide what they will do to take the last shot of the game.

The coach's job is to call the strategy, yet he has to do that with less-than-complete information and in a limited amount of time. Perhaps that feels eerily similar to your life as a leader.

He tells the players they will use their ace shooter Jimmy as a decoy and have someone else take the last shot. Despite the sound logic of this call, the boys don't put their hands in the middle of the huddle, shout "TEAM!" and then run onto the court. Instead, they stop leaning in, their shoulders sag and none of them is looking at the coach.

In my *Engagement* programs, I ask attendees what happened. They consistently say the boys don't buy in to the coach's strategy.

Because none of the boys in the movie offers a word of explanation, I ask attendees what makes them think the players have not bought into the coach's plan. They cite the disengagement they see, the body movement away from the coach, the break in eye contact, and the changes to the players' faces. That is, it is all about the body language they observe. And that is the first lesson of the Hoosiers huddle scene.

## BODY LANGUAGE

I have delivered hundreds of leadership programs to people from many cultures, and it is interesting that everyone sees exactly the same thing—the players' message of no buy-in—even though not a word of disagreement with the coach's call is spoken.

That is because whatever language you grew up speaking, it was your second language. Your first was body language, and you learned it from Mom. It is the most powerful language for every one of us and it is so powerful that it can overpower the spoken word. Here is an example of that.

Imagine sitting in someone's office and discussing something important to you. The monitor on their computer screen flashes to indicate an e-mail has been received. Your discussion partner shifts her eyes to the screen, simultaneously telling you to continue, that she is still listening.

Still listening? Really? How do you feel as this is happening?

I've asked that question of hundreds of keynote and workshop program attendees and the answers always sound like this: "No, she's not listening, and I'm feeling blown off and disrespected." Such is the power of body language, even in the face of contradictory words.

If you want to influence others to give their best, you'll have to be the best leader you can be and a major part of that is to be a great listener. Further, your body language must be congruent with your words. Those who look to you for leadership read body language every bit as well as you do. If your body language says something different from your words, they will believe your body language because, like you, body language is the most powerful language for them.

That is not to suggest that you should be self-conscious in the extreme; rather, it is to say that your words will not convince anyone if they are in conflict with your body language. Even more, the doubt and confusion such differences cause is dispiriting and will create sub-optimal results for everyone. There is a better way.

## JUST TELL THE TRUTH

If, for example, you don't have time to give your full attention to others, do the respectful thing and tell them you want to give them your full attention but can't do it right now. That applies to accepting telephone calls, checking e-mail, sneaking a peak at text messages, and anything else that tries to steal your attention. Make a date to meet when you can give them your full attention. That way, they will feel and appreciate your respect for them and will respond accordingly.

# CHAPTER 7

# You Said What?

*"You cannot truly listen to anyone and do
anything else at the same time."*

M. SCOTT PECK
PSYCHIATRIST AND AUTHOR OF THE ROAD LESS TRAVELED

L et's dig deeper into the Hoosiers huddle
scene. After the "no buy-in" moment, there
is a nine second exchange starting with the
coach asking the boys, "What's the matter with
you guys? What's the matter with you?" He is
answered by ace shooter Jimmy saying, "I'll make
it." That is followed by a long silence as we await
the coach's response.

In my keynotes and workshops, before I show
that nine seconds of film, I ask attendees to view
the scene differently, this time imagining they
are Jimmy. After watching the scene I ask if they
felt heard, if the coach listened, and the answer
is always "yes." They explain that they felt heard
because of the coach's eye contact, his leaning in to
listen, the change in his facial expression, the nod
of his head, the agreement with Jimmy, and the

subsequent change of strategy. All of those details of body language tell us the coach listened.

Eye contact shows that someone is focused on us. Leaning in tells us the person is putting energy into hearing us. A change in facial expression, even a subtle one, indicates the person is responding to what we say. A nod of the head and a change of mind are cues indicating someone has been listening to us, and we are all adept at perceiving these signals.

And we human beings like being listened to. We like it a lot. That is why *Engagement* Practice #3 is:

## ENGAGEMENT Practice #3

# Listen

To be clear, this is akin to Stephen Covey's principle from *The Seven Habits of Highly Effective People*: "Seek first to understand."[22] It requires listening solely for understanding. For many of us, though, that simply is not a habit.

We live in a fast-paced, jam-packed world and leaders so often have other people, events, and tasks tugging at their sleeves. At times, knee-jerk responses are all we can muster.

And because we are so busy, we aren't looking for more to do, and we do not want to take any longer than necessary to accomplish any task. That

frequently leads to our minds racing ahead or
aside while others are talking to us.

Sometimes we hear enough of the other person's
message to believe we understand, and then we
tune out as we formulate our response. Or our focus
remains elsewhere and our demeanor shows up as
impatience or lack of interest.

## POLAR OPPOSITES

Yet others know when we aren't being attentive,
and that leads to bad outcomes. To illustrate this
point, consider this pair of polar opposites.

A fellow by the name of Mr. Ibrahimi made
the news in Chicago[23] several years ago. In an
overnight rampage, he killed his wife, his wife's
sister, and his wife's mother. Oddly, after the
carnage, he video-recorded himself using his cell
phone. His short message was "I did it because
they didn't respect me."

This guy felt so disrespected—"dissed" in the
vernacular—that he became homicidal.

Clearly, most of us don't become violent over
feeling disrespected; however, every one of us
reacts negatively to feeling disrespected by others.
We may become passive-aggressive and refuse
to give our best. We may even refuse to have
anything to do with someone whom we believe
has disrespected us.

And disrespected is exactly how people feel when they are talking to someone who isn't listening.

If you are a leader and fail to listen to those who look to you for leadership, you can be confident they feel disrespected and they will react negatively. They will likely not give their best; they may disengage entirely and become a direct obstacle to success.

The polar opposite to Mr. Ibrahimi can be found in the words of David Oxberg, who said,

> *Being listened to is so close to being loved that most people cannot tell the difference.*[24]

Yes, it is that powerful. We human beings feel respected and cared about—even loved—when someone truly focuses on us as we are talking to them. We are moved by their undivided attention.

Of course, I'm not suggesting that all who look to you for leadership should fall in love with you; that is neither realistic nor even useful. But if you listen to your people by seeking solely to understand them, they will read that in your body language. They will recognize you aren't interrupting or hurrying them. They will feel your focus on them and will be moved in only the finest ways. They will feel your respect for them. The message that you care about them will come through loud and clear. And they will move to the right on the Discretionary Effort Continuum just because you listen.

Those who look to you for leadership want to be
inspired to give their best, and feeling your respect
for them has the power to drive that inspiration.
That power is described in the lyrics of the 1967
Aretha Franklin hit song "Respect":[25]

> *"What you want, baby I got.*
> *"What you need, you know I got it.*
> *"All I'm askin' is for a little . . .*
> *"R – E – S – P – E – C – T . . ."*

And one of the easiest ways to show that you
respect others is to simply listen to them.

Note that this is not a passive exercise; it is whole
body listening. Some call it empathic listening;
some call it active listening. Whatever the label, this
high-energy exercise requires all of your focus. And
it is worth that effort.

## TAKE TOO MUCH TIME?

Does it seem like conversations will take too long
if you listen solely to understand and don't use part
of the time the other person is talking to craft your
response? Actually, it is the most efficient use of
your discussion time.

While I was delivering a program in Halifax,
Nova Scotia, a CEO in attendance jumped on this
point. She said her greatest fear as a leader was
that yet another person would tug at her sleeve
saying, "Boss, got a minute?" The answer, of course,

was that she did have a minute, but rarely were these meetings completed that quickly. Indeed, she reported that some would take from thirty minutes to an hour—so, no, she did not "have a minute." Then she tried an experiment.

She reported that the next time an employee asked her that dreaded question, she brought the person into her office, closed the door, turned off the monitor of her computer, put her telephone ringer on silent, and focused solely on listening to that person. She reported that the meeting still didn't last just one minute, but it was complete in only five minutes. That is a significant improvement over the thirty to sixty minutes she had expected and dreaded.

And the story got better.

That CEO said the biggest time saver was that by following this procedure—eliminating distractions and listening attentively to those who wanted to talk to her—she stopped having the same conversation multiple times.

Sometimes, when people don't feel heard they will circle back and bring up the same issue again. If you experience that with your people, it is likely they are hoping that during this iteration of the conversation they will at last walk away feeling heard.

The Halifax CEO's story tells us that, to minimize time spent with the concerns and ideas of others, you must listen to them for understanding and do so with your full attention. When you do that, you'll gain a better understanding faster, your people will see that you respect them, and you'll only have the conversation once.

And all you have to do is follow *Engagement* Practice #3: Listen.

# CHAPTER 8

# It Isn't Safe to Play It Safe

*"You can either win the argument or you can have the relationship. You cannot have both."*

While driving between two of my CEO coaching sessions on a beautiful summer day with the convertible top down, I was listening to a program on the radio. A journalist was doing a series of reports on teen dating and in this report she was interviewing Michael, a thirteen-year-old 8th grader. She asked, "Michael, do you date?" He replied shyly, "Well, a little."

The reporter continued, "When you want to ask a girl out on a date, do you call her on the telephone?" Michael responded, "Nuh-uh."

"Well, how would you ask a girl out on a date?"

"I'd text her or send an e-mail."

"Why would you do it that way?" the reporter asked. When I heard Michael's answer, I stopped the car and wrote down what he said, word for word.

"I'd rather get rejected online. It's easier on the heart."

I've yet to find anyone who doesn't understand that.

Michael was indirectly saying he could deal with a girl saying no to his invitation. But he couldn't deal with hearing her laugh at him when she said no or perhaps he imagined some other sting he would prefer not to experience. He was protecting himself from the pain of rejection.

That isn't just a teenager thing. All of us naturally avoid pain whenever we can, and therefore, like Michael, we often do our best to play it safe. Sometimes that leads us to avoid having conflict conversations and that is a major impediment to accountability and success.

Brian Muldoon, author of *The Heart of Conflict*, gives clear definition to what makes conflict daunting for so many people. He explains,

> *Conflict forces us beyond our limits. It disturbs our sleep, rattles our cage, pushes us out of the nest, deprives us of comfort, makes us stand on our own two feet.*
>
> *So we avoid it, deny it, repress it, hang up on it, transfer it to the next department, refuse to answer letters, pretend not to see it, get*

*confused by it, and try to sleep through it. We just want it to go away.*

*[But c]onflict is not resolved through pretense or wishful thinking.*[26]

Muldoon describes the confrontation associated with conflict as "...hostile, intimidating, potentially dangerous."[27] No wonder, then, that, "Corporate managers are often more willing to terminate an unproductive employee than to confront him with the facts of his performance and set a deadline for improvement."[28]

Indeed, most people experience conflict as a threat to their very identity, which causes us to go into fight or flight mode. Muldoon once again:

*...when my [identity] is threatened, the powerful instincts of survival are invoked. At all costs we defend the "self" – not just the body, but the identity of which it is a part...we will fight harder for our ideas than for our actual corporeal survival.*[29]

*When we are in conflict...the only way out of it is to defeat the enemy. We just want to win.*[30]

Little wonder, then, that most of us expect a conflict conversation to be a bloody battle where somebody and perhaps everybody gets hurt. That's a powerful motivator to play it safe and avoid those conversations.

## WHEN WE TRY TO AVOID RISK

To be specific, when we try to avoid the risk of pain we expect to be caused by a conflict conversation, at times that leads us to avoid dealing with conflict at all. We attach to conflict the real or imagined threats to the relationship, concern over how we will be perceived, and whether we will be accepted or rejected. Yet there is a built-in contradiction in our avoidance.

Think of a conflict you've experienced, one you didn't deal with promptly. By ignoring it, did it go away? Chances are it did not. In fact, chances are when you finally dealt with the conflict, it had become far more difficult to handle—perhaps even more painful—than if you had addressed it right away. Muldoon, one last time: "But conflict doesn't go away. Generally, conflict gets worse until it gets noticed."[31] So there really is no safety in playing it safe.

## THE COST OF AVOIDANCE

In your leadership role, the penalty for failing to deal promptly with conflict multiplies. For example, a conflict between you and someone who looks to you for leadership leaves a cloud over that person's head and a cloud over your own. You both know it, too. You're not at your best and, for each of you, that creates a direct obstacle to getting more of what you want and less of what you don't want.

To take this farther, imagine the conflict between you and a follower who is failing to be accountable, giving less than his or her best. You can actually calculate the cost of someone acting in this way— being less productive, turning in a lower quality work product or failing to perform in a timely manner. The big cost, though, happens elsewhere.

A stunning article published on the Harvard Business Review Blog in 2012 titled "Are You Sure You're Not a Bad Boss?"[32] examined this issue. The authors looked at the 360-degree evaluations of over 30,000 leaders with an average of twelve respondents each. This was feedback rich in information about what motivates employees— and what dispirits them.

From this information, the authors constructed a list of the top ten factors that make for a bad boss. The number two factor was this: "Acceptance of mediocre performance in place of excellent results." Translation: "Boss, you let Bob get away with giving less than his best, with being unaccountable, and that just takes the wind out of my sails."

That is how others, especially top performers, experience such a situation. It is dispiriting. So the big cost of refusing to confront Bob and letting him get away with poor behavior is the effect it has on all of your top performers. At some point, they may begin giving less than their best. Eventually, they may find new employment in a place where they can count on their co-workers, which results in high-cost consequences for you.

That is why *Engagement* Practice #4 is:

## ENGAGEMENT Practice #4

# Deal With Conflict

To avoid negative results, we simply must have the discussion—the conflict conversation—with the underperformer and do it promptly. Yet many of us are conditioned by experience to dislike conflict conversations, so we avoid them. We fear the conversation itself as well as the adverse outcomes we imagine will develop. However, you have too much at stake to let conflict linger, which is why great leaders deal with conflict promptly.

### ENGAGING IN THE CONFLICT CONVERSATION

Having researched conflict resolution and consulted with a number of conflict resolution experts, it is clear to me that relationship safety is often at the core of the issue and is a primary driver of conflict avoidance. To aid in these necessary conversations in the face of such trepidation, a little help is called for, so the *Engagement* Rules for Safe Conflict are shown in Figure 3:

## ENGAGEMENT

# Rules for Safe Conflict

- Abandon winning
- Listen
- Stay focused on the goal

**FIGURE 3:** The Engagement Rules for Safe Conflict

In this context, "safe" is defined as both resolving the conflict and preserving the relationship.

Note that this construct is not about the nuts and bolts of the conversation; it is about the attitude we bring to it and how to foster a positive outcome.[33]

## ABANDON WINNING

A conflict conversation is never about your worth as a person, the puffing of your ego, your place in the pecking order, your status as leader, the superior quality of your ideas or your remarkable intelligence. Sadly, this kind of "it's all about how I see myself and how others see me" anchor permeates many conflict conversations and it often spawns behavior that is defensive and even offensive (in both senses of the word). Indeed, this is where the conflict conversation train so often flies off the track. It is imperative to avoid this dynamic if you are to have a constructive conversation.

You know you're hip-deep in making the discussion about self-worth, though, when you have gone back and forth in the conversation two or three times, you're about to make another retort and suddenly realize that you can't remember the topic of the conversation. You're using every lever you can find, fair or otherwise, to win the argument. Feel familiar? Well, an inherent self-sabotage exists in doing that.

A win-lose outcome most often devolves into lose-lose. That is because when someone wins the argument, someone else loses, and something bad is almost certain to happen from that.

When you lose the argument you may feel marginalized or be made to feel "less than." Resentment grows and it is resentment that damages relationships, making it difficult to cooperate fully in the future. And it is the reason why, when one person wins the argument, eventually both lose.

So, the clarification of "Abandon Winning" is this:

> You can either win the argument or you can have the relationship. You cannot have both.

Don't imagine this means that you should simply cave in, because that just isn't so. It means that you should make your case vigorously and with as much passion as is appropriate. Do it, though, in search of the best outcome, rather than to win the argument *and make the other guy lose.*

If you want to have a safe conflict conversation, abandon having to win the argument. My promise to you is that you will be okay and your ego will remain intact.

## LISTEN

This relates to *Engagement* Practice #3: Listen. It is important because when we feel listened to we feel safe. We feel respected. We aren't compelled to enter into verbal combat to dominate or to protect ourselves.

As an example, imagine you and I are having a conflict conversation. When you fully listen to me, I feel respected and safe, and I don't have a need to attack or defend. The bigger magic is that when you fully listen to me, you probably don't have a need to attack or defend, either. The simple act of listening creates safety for all that is critical to a productive, constructive conversation.

So, to have a safe conflict conversation, listen solely for understanding.

## STAY FOCUSED ON THE GOAL

The real goals of a conflict conversation should be to resolve the conflict and to enhance the relationship so we can work together even better tomorrow. To that end, having a safe conflict conversation means focusing on those two things.

To use a metaphor, we get on the same side of the table and examine what we have. We acknowledge that each of us has passion about the issue and each believes s/he has the best solution or is right. Then we work cooperatively to find the best outcome.

During a program I conducted in Denver, a CEO said that when he has a conflict conversation he physically moves from behind his desk and goes to the same side as his conversation partner. That way, they are literally as well as metaphorically on the same side. His is a pretty good idea.

Sometimes no middle-ground solution appears, and only one person's idea will carry the day. In an imaginary conflict conversation between you and me, if we don't battle to win the argument and make the other lose, if we fully listen to one another, and if we focus on resolving the conflict and enhancing our relationship, I will feel okay if your idea carries the day. I may still like my idea better and I will likely still think I was right, but I will feel respected and able to go your way. We've kept our relationship intact, perhaps even strengthened it, and we will be ready to move forward together, each giving our best.

Taking this to a poetic level, the 13th century Sufi poet, Rumi, wrote a poem entitled "There Is A Field." Its first few lines are:

*Out beyond ideas of*
*Wrong-doing and right-doing*
*There is a field.*
*I'll meet you there.*[34]

As you read those words again, see the field
in your mind's eye. Imagine your conflict
conversation taking place in that field. Go
ahead—read it again.

In that place it isn't about wrong-doing or right-
doing, good or bad, smart or dumb, or any of
the vast array of polar opposites our defensive
minds create to win arguments. If we follow
the *Engagement* Rules for Safe Conflict, safe
resolution will likely prevail.

Let's make this actionable for you. Think about
conflicts with your name on them. They can be in
any area of your life, but leaving them unresolved
is an obstacle to your getting more of what you
want and less of what you don't want.

Make a note of those conflicts as a reminder to
circle back to them. Perhaps one or two just came
to mind, so note them in the margin of this page.
Then, one at a time, have the conversations.

That is what great leaders do.

# CHAPTER 9

# Great Leaders

*"If your actions inspire others to dream more, learn more, do more and become more, you are a leader."*

JOHN QUINCY ADAMS, SIXTH PRESIDENT OF THE UNITED STATES

Often in my interactive keynote addresses and in each of my workshop programs, I ask a volunteer to talk about a great leader in his life. It can be a parent, a teacher, a coach, a clergy person, a boss—it doesn't matter, as long as he had a one-to-one relationship with this leader. I then ask the volunteer to explain what made that individual a great leader for him. I also have the person talk about his response—his followership—to that person's leadership.

The inspirational stories they've told are wide ranging and I have learned of the most amazing leaders, people who were able to draw the very best from others and accomplish great things.

It is striking that I hear three types of comments so consistently about these great leaders that it's impossible to miss the pattern. They are the core characteristics we human beings look for and respond to in a leader; the presence of these traits almost always defines a great leader. To illustrate, here is the story a leadership program attendee (we'll call him Mike) told about a great leader in his life.

Mike worked for Frank for several years. A vice-president of his company, Frank was in charge of both domestic and international sales and his weighty responsibilities constantly demanded his attention.

The attributes Mike used to describe Frank as his great leader were captured with these bullet points:

- He mentored me.

- He cared about me.

- He gave me tough assignments.

- In conversations, he asked lots of questions.

- He respected me.

- He was very demanding.

I poked at several of his points, first asking Mike how he knew that Frank cared about him. He said that in so many of their conversations, Frank asked about Mike and how things were going for him, both in his company functions and outside of work. Mike reported that Frank was interested in him as a person, not just as an employee.

When asked how he knew that Frank respected him, Mike said his boss listened carefully to what he said. Frank always seemed to give serious consideration to Mike's ideas. Most of the time when Mike asked for direction from Frank, his boss would ask Mike what he thought; then Frank usually advised Mike to use his best judgment.

When I asked Mike about Frank being very demanding, he said Frank always gave him the toughest assignments. I asked what that meant to him and Mike replied, "When he would hand one of the really challenging jobs to me, he would usually say something like, 'I know you can handle this.' That meant the world to me." He also said that when he had accomplished a difficult task, Frank was quick with some form of "atta boy."

In the second part of the exercise, Mike talked about how he responded to Frank's leadership, saying, "I would have walked through walls for him. I didn't want to let him down, and I did whatever it took." When I asked Mike if Frank would have described him as a high performer relative to his capabilities, like every attendee I have asked, he answered, "Definitely!" The exclamation point reflects the enthusiasm that always comes with this answer.

Mike's story about Frank fits perfectly the characteristics I hear consistently from leadership program attendees about their great leaders. I have captured these under the banner of The Core of Great Leadership:

> ## ENGAGEMENT
>
> # THE CORE OF GREAT LEADERSHIP
>
> Be *fully alive*, right here, right now
>
> —
>
> Demonstrate that you care
>
> —
>
> Validate: Let them know you believe in them

**FIGURE 3:** The Core of Great Leadership

## BE *FULLY ALIVE*, RIGHT HERE, RIGHT NOW

We know when people are fully present with us. We also know when they're only giving us a portion of their attention. Great leaders, though, always show up with their full presence when they are with us.

I tested that characteristic with Mike about how Frank showed up by asking this question: "Even though Frank was very busy and had weighty things on his mind, when he was with you, he was fully present with you and no place else. True or false?" Mike's enthusiastic answer was "Absolutely!"

And that kind of strong affirmation is how every *Engagement* keynote and workshop attendee has responded to that question. That's "every" as in 100 percent.

These busy leaders manage to be fully present with those who look to them for leadership, even as a multitude of things vie for their attention. That means everything to their followers, who feel cared about and respected, even honored due to that complete focus. That in turn influences followers to give their best. That is what great leaders do. Always.

To focus this more sharply, there is a pair of Zen questions that are always answered the same way. The first is "Where are you?" The answer is "Here." You are always "here" and you are never any other place. And that is where great leaders show up with those who look to them for leadership.

The second question is "What time is it?" The answer to that question is "Now." You are always "here" and the time is always "now," which brings us to:

## ENGAGEMENT Practice #5

# Be Here Now

Showing up in that way is required for great leadership and to produce the corresponding great followership of others. That is where great leadership always happens. Indeed, that is where and when all of your life happens. It never happens anywhere else or at any other time.

## DEMONSTRATE THAT YOU CARE

Recall the Towers Watson finding from Chapter 2:

> The number one driver of employee engagement is the belief that senior [leadership] is sincerely interested in employee well being.

While many things can influence people to give more of themselves, the biggest driver is the message from the leader that s/he cares. That sense of caring causes people to shift to the right—toward greater engagement—on The Discretionary Effort Continuum, this because they want to.

Not surprisingly, great leaders sincerely care about their people and find their own ways to demonstrate that. Recall that Mike reported he knew that Frank cared about him because Frank asked about how things were going for him both at work and outside his business life. That demonstration of caring about him had a powerful, positive impact on Mike, just as your demonstration of caring will on your followers.

## VALIDATE – LET THEM KNOW YOU BELIEVE IN THEM

Mike was clear about being validated by his boss. Frank was always letting Mike know—both directly and indirectly—that he saw something in him, that he believed in him.

Sometimes it was slightly indirect, like the example Mike offered about difficult jobs and Frank saying that Mike could handle it. Other times Frank stayed out of the way, relying on Mike to use his own judgment. That gave indirect confirmation to Mike that Frank had confidence in him. Sometimes Frank's validation of Mike was a simple "atta boy." In all cases, Mike got the validating message and was positively motivated.

It is interesting to note that in describing how they responded to their great leader, many of the people who have shared their great leader story described having done things they had never before imagined they could do. They reported that they would do whatever it takes, but would never let down their great leader. Such is the power of presence, caring and validation.

Perhaps you have noticed these engagement practices are specific ways to demonstrate that you care. Always remember that is a primary driver for people to want to give their best.

## LEADING A VISTAGE CEO GROUP

Vistage International, Inc., formerly TEC—
The Executive Committee—is a worldwide
organization conducting local executive roundtables
for the purpose of driving success. It harnesses
the power of group members to help one another
mount challenges, seize opportunities to best
advantage and counsel one another as a peer
advisory board. Along with monthly meetings
come regular one-on-one coaching sessions with
the group chairman.

When I began chairing Vistage CEO roundtables,
I had not been a member of a Vistage group, and,
except for what I learned in a few days of training,
I didn't even know what a Vistage meeting should
look like.

Immediately following the training to become
a group chairman I took over a group for a
veteran group chairman who was retiring. He had
arranged for a speaker to present to the group at
my first meeting, so the first part of the meeting
day was conducted by the speaker. He presented
his half-day workshop and then departed. After
lunch, we held our afternoon executive session.

At the meeting's end, the group members left and
as I was gathering my meeting materials, I came
upon a note the morning presenter had left for
me. It read, "You are the best group chairman I've
seen in action in three years."

Given this was my first meeting and I hadn't much of a clue what was going on, I thought, "What a bunch of nonsense!" I tossed down the note, finished cleaning up, and left.

When I arrived home that evening, I started putting away the meeting materials and came upon the note once again. The presenter had seemed like an honest guy and I thought that, clearly, what he wrote wasn't literally true. Both he and I knew that, so what could he have meant?

After giving it some thought, I realized that he saw I could be good—the best he'd seen in action in three years—if I gave everything I had in me to lead my Vistage groups to the best of my ability. Not surprisingly, I spent the next ten years working to live up to what he saw in me.

Significantly, that note has found a permanent place in the top left drawer of my desk.

We human beings are dramatically affected when someone we regard as an authority figure, as a leader, sees something in us. Validation from that person can mean so much. And because of that speaker's validation and belief in me, I became a better facilitator and leader of my groups.

Remember that those who look to you for leadership want your validation, your belief in them. They want to know you see a spark of greatness in them.

## "BELIEVE IN ME"

The impact that speaker had on me was profound. Yet at the same time, it was ordinary in the sense that people commonly respond to validation in such a strongly positive way. That I have kept his note all these years is common to what others do when they receive such validation.

To informally test the importance of validation, I have asked attendees at my presentations to raise their hands if they have kept a validating note from someone who was a leader in their life. Between one-third and two-thirds of the hands go up at every event. Those notes of validation are keepers.

You are a leader. Those looking to you for leadership need your validation, your belief in them. They want to know you see something noteworthy in them. So decide now: To whom will you write a note expressing your belief in them? Make a list in the margin of this page of the people who look to you for leadership and write them a validating note. Your verbal validation of them has impact, but a note is a gift that keeps on giving—just as that speaker's note did for me.

To be clear, this is only about telling the truth. If you don't mean it, don't say it.

We're all overly busy, so it is easy to allow opportunities to give validation to slip away. So, make your list now, and then start writing those notes. Handwrite them on a card or a blank piece of paper or even on a sticky note. The paper doesn't matter; the message does. And because this is a personal note from a person to a person, don't even think of using e-mail or texting.

And if you really want to have impact, write notes to your children. If you have grandchildren, write notes to them, too.

Validation is what great leaders do.

And this gets even better.

A fundamental of human behavior is: See leader—Emulate leader. We human beings naturally adjust ourselves to the style, the manner and the experience we have of our leaders. That is why the Core of Great Leadership is so powerful. When you show up fully present and communicate your caring and belief in your people, they will begin to emulate you and there will be a multiplier effect that reverberates throughout your organization.

# CHAPTER 10

# Where You Set the Bar

*"Good enough isn't good enough."*

ANONYMOUS

While it has risen 15 percent from a low of 54 percent in 2008 to the 2014 rate of 69 percent, the on-time (four year) graduation rate from the Chicago Public High Schools remains abysmally low.[35] In stark contrast to that is the Urban Prep Charter Academy for Young Men, which has had an on-time graduation rate of 100 percent since its doors opened in 2002.[36]

And the story gets even better.

One hundred percent of the Urban Prep Charter Academy graduates go on to four-year colleges and universities and the school and the students have racked up grants and scholarships totaling millions of dollars. This is, indeed, a high-performing group of young people.

Here is one more key piece of information: The Urban Prep Charter Academy is located in the Englewood neighborhood of Chicago. Due to a very high crime rate, it is one of the toughest, deadliest South Side neighborhoods in the city. And prior to entering Urban Prep only 4 percent of the students can read at grade level.

For most kids in such an environment, the future would be quite perilous. Yet the young men at the Urban Prep Charter Academy are well-prepared for successful, productive and satisfying lives.

How can this school in such a tough neighborhood achieve these outstanding results? That question was asked by a journalist in 2010 in an interview with Tim King, CEO of the Urban Prep Charter Academies.[37] King answered by saying the Academy's success hinges on three things:

1.  We insist upon excellence

2.  We provide the tools to succeed

3.  We have an extended school day and an extended school year

## 1. WE INSIST UPON EXCELLENCE

To be clear, that doesn't mean every student has to be the highest performing student in the world. Rather, it means each student has to be the best student that young man can be. It is entirely about personal best.

The many stories I've heard about a teacher coming to an inner-city school and working miracles with the kids share this fact: In each case, the teacher told the students they will clear the bar "up here." They tell the kids they are too important to not clear the bar, and that the teacher will not allow failure. And, no, the bar won't be lowered for anyone. They're expected to clear it "up here." And they do.

When it comes to bars, people will clear the bar where the leader sets it. If you set the bar low, your people will clear it, but they will clear the bar low. There is no satisfaction nor are there high-fives for clearing a low bar. It is boring and uninspiring. On the other hand, if you set the bar high, people will strive to clear the bar high and there will be high-fives all around.

So, do what great leaders do:

## ENGAGEMENT Practice #6
# Set the Bar High

That is exactly what the Urban Prep Charter Academy for Young Men does and that provides the cornerstone for motivating its students to perform at their best. In fact, the highly inspirational, multi-point Urban Prep Creed includes this bar-setting statement:

*"We are college bound."*[38]

At Urban Prep the insistence on excellent performance is not in the least about what that excellence will do for teachers or for the school. Rather, the focus is entirely on caring enough about the students becoming the very best versions of themselves, of achieving their personal best. That is why the bar is set high.

Recall that Chapter 2 emphasized caring about those who look to you for leadership. When you do that, they get the message and respond with their best. Insisting on your people's best *because they are too important to be less than their best* is a powerful way to show that you care.

Another way to insist upon excellence is by making it clear that "Good enough isn't good enough."

There is a tyranny inherent in accepting "good enough;" it rationalizes and accepts mediocre performance. Indeed, it is a direct impediment to people being the best version of themselves. It is also an obstacle to their getting more of what they want and less of what they don't want.

When your people give their best, it most certainly will redound to you. However, that is not the reason to set the bar high. The reason—the "True North" why—is for them to be their best.

*So insist on excellence,* just as they do at The Urban Prep Charter Academy for Young Men.

## 2. WE PROVIDE THE TOOLS TO SUCCEED

The second point Tim King noted as a driver of top student performance is providing the tools to succeed. That includes the school itself, the computer labs, the skilled faculty, the insistence on parental involvement and more. Those teenagers have what they need in order to learn and excel and succeed.

It is possible you feel confident that those who look to you for leadership have the tools to succeed, too, but test your notion by doing this exercise. Go to one of your direct reports, perhaps in a mentoring session, and ask this question:

*"What is the one thing which, if you had it, would make all the difference?"* [17]

You may be surprised at the response.

Remember, your direct reports have their hands on things you do not. That means that they have certain knowledge and understanding you can't possibly have. They may know of a software module or a tool or a different workspace layout that would boost productivity or quality of performance.

So, listen (as in: *Engagement* Practice #3) to what that person says and take appropriate action. Then have the same conversation with the rest of your direct reports, one by one. By doing this, you will open the doors to improvement in productivity and success for everyone.

Here is an example of how that can look and the possibility for improvement you might expect from such a conversation.

Captain D. Michael Abrashoff (USN, retired) took command of the USS Benfold in June, 1997 and tells the story in his book *It's Your Ship: Management Techniques from the Best Damn Ship in the Navy.*[39] The Benfold had been an average performing ship with a typical turnover rate of crewmembers. Sailors would serve their tour and then transfer to another assignment, taking their knowledge and skills with them. That left the Benfold constantly short of high-performing, knowledgeable hands on board, so Abrashoff took it upon himself to change that dynamic and turn the Benfold into a high-performing ship.

To accomplish that, he began a program he called "Ask-Listen-Respond." He approached each sailor on the Benfold one at a time with get-to-know-you questions. Then he asked the key question: "What ideas do you have for improvement?"

That was the "ask" phase.

The next step was to listen (as in: *Engagement* Practice #6—Listen). Abrashoff took the sailors and their ideas seriously, framing it this way:

> *...I vowed to treat every encounter with every person on the ship as the most important thing at that moment.*[40]

Recall from Chapter 6 the positive results that listening creates. That is exactly what happened aboard the USS Benfold.

The third phase of Captain Abrashoff's program was to respond. Sometimes it was as simple as saying, "Make it so, sailor." Other times research was needed before answering, but Captain Abrashoff always responded promptly and appropriately.

The results were amazing. Statistics showed the USS Benfold became one of the highest-performing ships in the U.S. Navy. It won the prestigious Spokane Trophy in 1997 as the most combat-ready ship in the entire Pacific Fleet.

In fact, the Benfold became a model of naval performance and efficiency. It showed huge cost savings and had the highest gunnery score in the Pacific Fleet due to its highly motivated, top-performing crew.

The Navy had pages of names of sailors who wanted to get posted on the USS Benfold, but they couldn't get assigned there because the sailors aboard loved being on that ship so much that they refused to leave.

There are many leadership lessons that can be drawn from Captain Abrashoff and the USS Benfold experience and the Ask-Listen-Respond program is one of the most powerful. Recall that people who look to you for leadership have hands-on experience you do not have and they know things you cannot know. They can and will provide valuable ideas for improvement—and all you have to do is ask, listen and respond.

Asking what your people think has an added benefit. When you ask for their ideas, people get the message loud and clear that their leader respects and cares about them. They respond by engaging in their jobs at a higher level, perhaps even giving their A-game. Here is another example to support this point.

## WHAT DO YOU THINK?

In doing research for a keynote presentation for a trade association on the subject of employee engagement, I had the opportunity to interview business-owner members of the association. I also interviewed quite a few employees of these business owners.

In my conversations with employees, I asked a series of open-ended questions similar to those Captain Abrashoff asked. They had to do with what was going well, what they'd like to improve, what their pet peeves were, and so on. And one of the responses repeated often was "I want them to ask me what I think." Indeed, this was usually expressed with a tone of frustration.

Because people believe they have good ideas, they want their bosses to ask about them. They want the feeling of respect that such asking connotes. They want things to be better in their shops and believe that their ideas will help that to happen. They want to be taken seriously.

Too often, the "What do you think?" question doesn't get asked, leaving employees feeling like they are being kept in the dark due to one-way communication and, worse, feeling as though leadership has no interest in them. That can destroy morale, engagement, and performance. It is an obstacle to everyone getting more of what they want and less of what they don't want.

Obstacles can be overcome and people can find motivation to fully engage simply by leaders using the Ask-Listen-Respond formula.

## 3. WE HAVE AN EXTENDED SCHOOL DAY AND AN EXTENDED SCHOOL YEAR

*(back to the Urban Prep Charter Academy For Young Men in Chicago)*

That is the third reason Tim King provided to explain the great achievements his students and school are having. These kids work long and they work hard to achieve academic excellence. While extending working hours may not make sense in your business environment, it surely does at the Urban Prep Charter Academy.

The interview with Tim King was both interesting and eye opening, yet the most poignant moment of the journalist's report came during her interview with a sophomore at the Urban Prep Charter Academy. She said to this fifteen-year-old that she had checked on him and learned that he just got by in middle school, but he was getting a grade of A in every class at Urban Prep. Why, she asked, was he doing so well? That student didn't skip a beat as he answered, "Because here the teachers care about me."

He didn't talk about insistence on excellence or tools to succeed or the extended school day and year. His instant response was focused on being cared about. This is powerful stuff, and it can be life changing. Note that a colleague in Atlanta who does volunteer work at an inner city high school asked the same question of some high-performing students there and received the same answer: "Because here the teachers care about me," word-for-word the same as the answer given by the student interviewed at the Urban Prep Charter Academy for Young Men in Chicago.

Back once again to the Towers Watson organization report detailed in Chapter 2:

> *The number one driver of employee engagement is the belief that senior [leadership] is sincerely interested in employee well being.*

The action dynamic created with high school kids and with the people who look to you for leadership is the same and can be stated this way:

"You care about me, so I care about you. And the last thing I'd ever want to do is to let you down. I'll do whatever it takes."

# CHAPTER 11

# Just Stories in Our Heads

*"'I can't' has never been a part of my vocabulary."*

WILMA RUDOLPH
THREE-TIME OLYMPIC GOLD MEDALIST
1960 SUMMER OLYMPIC GAMES, ROME, ITALY

People in positions of leadership typically possess a can-do attitude and often believe they can do anything they make up their minds to do. That positive attitude has helped them to create the level of success they have achieved, yet this assumption often goes unexamined.

While all that positive thinking is going on, something insidious is happening in our environment. The world is conveying messages about what *cannot* be done and these "I can't" messages are drummed into our heads in ways we don't recognize. We simply don't have any sense of how we become controlled by them or the consequences that lie in wait.

Through my years of chairing CEO roundtables, I saw how that can play out to sabotage success. For example, one CEO painted a picture about what he wanted to do with his company. He had a plan that was elegant and seemed to be well thought out. Then quite unknowingly, he did things that prevented the very success that he sought.

In dealing with this kind of thing in our executive roundtables, we found that time after time, a key component of failure was an unrecognized belief that, "I can't do that," with "can't" meaning "not able."

For our purposes here, the source of self-limiting notions doesn't matter; however, the impact of those notions matters a great deal, and so it is vital to:

## ENGAGEMENT Practice #7

# Deal With Reality

It is an imperative to deal with reality-not the story about reality that may be clanging around inside your head, yet doesn't exist anywhere else in the universe.

Here is an example that gives definition to this.

## OLYMPIC HEROINE

Wilma Rudolph had infantile paralysis and spent the first twelve years of her life in leg braces. All that time, though, she idolized her older sister, who became a high school basketball star. Wilma wanted to be just like her sister.

When Wilma no longer needed the braces, she dedicated herself to basketball and, in fact, just a few years later became a high school star.

Somewhere along the line, someone realized Wilma could run fast—extremely fast. She met the right people and trained with the same dedication she brought to being like her sister. Amazingly, she was selected for the U.S. Olympic team and went to the 1956 Summer Olympics in Melbourne, Australia. She came home with a bronze medal for the 4 X 100-meter relay. Four years later, she made even more Olympic history.

In the 1960 Summer Olympic Games in Rome, Italy, Wilma Rudolph was entered in three races. She won the 100-meter run with a record-breaking time of 11.0 seconds. To put that into perspective, as of the time of this writing, the women's Olympic record is 10.49 seconds, set by Florence Griffith-Joyner in 1988.

Later that week, Rudolph ran in the 200-meter event and won that race with a time of 23.5 seconds. At the end of the week, she competed in the 4 X 100-meter relay, the same race for which she'd won a bronze medal four years earlier. This time she and her teammates won the gold.

Wilma Rudolph came away from the 1960 Rome Olympics with three gold medals, something no woman had ever done before. All of that was achieved by a woman who spent the first twelve years of her life in leg braces.

When asked how she was able to accomplish so much, given her shaky start, she said, "*I can't*' has never been a part of my vocabulary." Translated for our purposes, she dealt with reality, not a story that might have seeped into her head about what she could not do.

Clearly, no athlete wins Olympic gold medals by saying "I can't." The same is true for the rest of us regarding the lofty goals we set for ourselves.

## AN ENABLING EXERCISE

A worthy exercise is to sit quietly for a while and ask, "What am I telling myself that I can't do?"

Perhaps you're telling yourself you can't have the success you say you want, that you can't be an industry leader or have the financial security you long to have. Maybe you're telling yourself you can't have the family dynamics you want or the life balance you want. You get the idea.

The world constantly puts these "I can't" notions into our heads, and we don't know that it is happening. It takes a concerted effort to see them for what they are—self-limiting notions that unknowingly became planted in our minds. The trick lies in uncovering these notions. When we do that, they instantly shift from "I can't" stories to "I will" or "I won't" decisions, and you will know every time which is the right path for you to choose.

When you do this exercise, resist the temptation to tell yourself you don't have any "I can't" stories, only "I will" and "I won't" stories, because that simply isn't useful to you in this process. Instead, proceed with the assumption that an obstacle is just waiting for you to expose it for the fraud that it is.

If you get stuck doing this exercise, write down these words:

> *I can't think of any "I can't" stories, and my resistance is...*

and then complete the sentence. You may find that liberating.

Take 15 minutes and jot down any self-limiting story that comes to mind. Let your mind wander to what gets in your way anywhere in your life. Go ahead—do it now.

Did you find something valuable for yourself? If not, try this again another day, just because this can be so helpful. And be clear that this exercise is like the toothpaste that won't go back in the tube. Once you know about the self-limiting story, you can't unknow it. Rather, it will be up to you to make the best decision for yourself.

## ASK OTHERS

Once you've succeeded in doing this, offer this exercise to the people who look to you for leadership. A good time might be during a mentoring session. Ask what they are telling themselves they cannot do, something that limits them. To spark a rich conversation, use yourself as an example. Tell the "I can't" story you uncovered about yourself and then explain what you are doing about it. Your being vulnerable in that way will allow others to feel safe to speak freely. It will also drive trust between you.

Great leaders deal with reality, not the stories about reality they may be telling themselves and others. Modeling that for those who look to you for leadership can unlock the greatness inside them. And it surely will free you to even greater success.

# CHAPTER 12

# What They
# Need You to Be

*"I can't tell you how hard it will be for me if you
lose it."*

FROM SIX DAYS, SEVEN NIGHTS
BUENA VISTA/TOUCHSTONE PICTURES, 1998

C aptain Richard Phillips was the skipper of
the merchant ship MV Maersk Alabama
in 2009. The ship was steaming from
Salalah, Oman, en route to Mombasa, Kenya,
when it was boarded by Somali pirates 600 miles
off the Somali coast. That was the first pirate
hijacking of an American flagship in more than
200 years. The 2013 movie *Captain Phillips*[41]
recounts the events of the hijacking. You'll find
many lessons for leaders embedded in this film.

The Alabama's crew members were armed with
a signal flare gun and faced AK-47-wielding
pirates. It was Captain Phillips's duty in this
armament imbalance to protect his twenty-man

crew and his vessel. Key to that was preventing panic and ensuring the men worked as a team for everyone's safety.

The movie portrays Phillips addressing his crew from the bridge of the Alabama via intercom as the pirates are boarding his ship. He tells them,

> *Listen up. We have been boarded by four armed pirates. You know the drill. We stay hidden no matter what. I don't want any hostages. We stay locked down until help arrives. No one comes out until you hear the non-duress password from me, which is "suppertime." If the pirates find you, remember, you know the ship; they don't. Make them feel like they're in charge, but keep them away from the important things like the generator and the engine controls. Stick together and we'll be all right. Good luck.*

Now imagine you are a member of that crew. How would you feel if your captain, your leader—the person with the plan who is supposed to keep you safe—were to fall apart instead? What would happen to your confidence, your sense of safety? What about your willingness to work with shipmates for everyone's safety?

All would surely be damaged. You might start operating solely to protect yourself and forget about everything and everyone else. Cooperation among the crew would suffer and, in the case of the Alabama crew, the results could have been terrible.

Every individual and team will come upon difficult times. Some may be life threatening—literally, in this example and among military teams, and figuratively for teams and companies facing severe crises. As a leader, your job is to keep your people calm, focused and working together for the best outcome.

Just as in Captain Phillips leading his crew, your people need leadership from you. Therefore, you must:

## ENGAGEMENT Practice #8

# Be Their Confident Captain

That doesn't mean you have to have all the best answers all the time. Everyone who looks to you for leadership knows that simply isn't possible. Nor does it mean that you have to be foolishly Pollyanna-like in your attitude. When the reality is that things are grave, it is appropriate to be serious.

Here is what it does mean: You must keep yourself together. You may not have been told this when you agreed to become the leader, but the day that shift occurred you gave up the right to fall apart in front of your people. Sure, you can lose it for a few moments at home or in private if you must. But never lose it in front of your people or in circumstances that might be reported to those who look to you for leadership. They need you to be their confident captain. In a crisis, everything turns on that.

## QUALITY MOVEMENT

W. Edwards Deming is considered by many to be the father of the Total Quality Management movement that was a huge initiative in the 1980s.

Deming had gone to Japan after World War II and taught quality management principles there at a time when nobody in American industry would listen to his ideas. Japan had been devastated by a decade of war and much of what its companies produced in the late 1940s and early 1950s could charitably be called "junk." Deming changed that.

He brought the engineering and psychological tools to Japanese companies that helped shift Japan to become a world leader in quality and an economic powerhouse. His teaching included his fourteen points as well as his fundamental principles.

One of those principles was driving fear out of the workplace.[42] That is critical because it is impossible to sustain giving our best when we are fearful for our place, our security and our tomorrow.

# BE CONFIDENT THINGS WILL BE SET RIGHT

Your confidence must lie in your belief that things will be set right. Your people need to know with certainty that together you will find the best way forward. They need to know you believe in them, and that together as a team, you will create successful outcomes.

Figure 3 in Chapter 9 speaks to what great leaders do. One of them is to validate your people—see their greatness and let them know you believe in them. A time of crisis provides an ideal—even critical—opportunity to express your belief in them, to let them know they are exactly the right people to find the way out of difficult circumstances. And they need to hear that message directly from you, and often.

Be their confident captain. Always.

# CHAPTER 13

# Binary

*"Failure is not an option."*

GENE KRANZ'S CHARACTER
*APOLLO 13*, UNIVERSAL PICTURES, 1995

The Apollo 13 mission was the third attempt to land men on the moon, explore its surface and collect moon rocks, then bring the specimens back to Earth.

On the way to the moon, a catastrophic equipment failure of the spacecraft put the lives of the three astronauts onboard in mortal danger. Quickly, the mission shifted from bringing home moon rocks to just getting the men back to Earth alive.

This happened at a time when we had relatively primitive tools for engineering a complex mission such as this, compared with today's capabilities. Indeed, your smartphone has more computing power than the computers that guided any of the Apollo missions. Figuring out how to keep the men alive long enough to bring them safely back to Earth involved slide rules and intricate and daringly untried solutions using materials not designed for the required tasks.

One key challenge was to ensure that the astronauts would have sufficient electrical power to bring about a safe re-entry to the Earth. In a meeting with NASA scientists and engineers, Gene Kranz, mission director, confronted them with the need to find a way—even in the face of having poor tools and no preparation for such a task. In the movie *Apollo 13*, Kranz is depicted as concluding the meeting by saying what has since become a staple of focused intention: "Failure is not an option."[43]

Think about the impact of that sentence—that attitude—in the context of that fateful moment, rather than with the often-glib use of the sentence today. Imagine yourself as one of the scientists facing a task so daunting, so unknown, that no one had ever thought about such a dilemma before, much less found a solution. What would such a declaration as Kranz's say to you?

Surely it would speak to *Engagement* Practice #8: Kranz was clearly being their confident captain. And it says more. It speaks to commitment.

To be committed is an absolute, quite like being pregnant: You either are or you are not; there is no middle ground. All-in at 100 percent. It is the only way any of us can commit. So, for example, if one of your direct reports tells you he or she is pretty committed to the new project, it is exactly the same as not being committed.

Indeed, to succeed to the fullest extent possible, you must be committed. That is true in part because a lack of commitment will result in your performing at less than your best.

But an even greater negative impact can and likely will happen. Remember that people always emulate their leader. So if you are not all-in, those who look to you for leadership will see or sense your lack of commitment and will emulate you. Once again, you lead by example, whether by intention or by accident.

So, do what great leaders do:

## ENGAGEMENT Practice #9

# Commit

Randy Pausch was an enormously popular computer science professor at Carnegie Mellon University. He contracted pancreatic cancer and has subsequently died.

While he was still fairly strong he gave his last lecture to hundreds of people and talked about many things, one of which was obstacles. He had them just like everyone else and his metaphor for his obstacles was brick walls. What he had to say about that was stunning: "The brick walls are there to show you how badly you want something."[44]

Do you imagine that the brick walls in your life are there to torment you? They are not. They are there for another purpose, one that Pausch was clear about: They are there to test you, to find out if you really mean what you say about your goals and your success. If you are to succeed, you'll have to commit.

## PROMISE TO YOURSELF

Be clear that committing is primarily about your promise to yourself. You are "all in" for what you say you want. You've abandoned the idea of waiting for success to drop into your lap from out of the blue.

Commitment requires full ownership and a sincere pledge to yourself to do whatever is necessary to achieve success—to live your "True North." That is how you will get more of what you want and less of what you don't want. Indeed, it is the only way.

Commitment resides at the intersection of good intentions and deliberate actions. What is your commitment to *you*?

# CHAPTER 14

# Making a Difference

*"In a gentle way, you can shake the world."*

MAHATMA GANDHI

I was deep in thought as I walked along the beautiful white sand beach early on my seventh morning on the island. I had kept to myself and actually had not talked to anyone for six days because this visit wasn't a vacation; it was a personal retreat.

I had founded and then run my industrial water treatment company for twenty-five years. Over the years, I experienced many successes, faced many challenges, and found great joy along the way. But the last few years proved to be less satisfying than earlier years and it became clear I had to move on, so I sold the company to a regional competitor.

Unfortunately, the sale process dragged on for a long time and that process turned into an unhappy time for me. My heart was no longer in the business, yet I had to continue to run it through the sale process and hold things together to the end. I did what had to be done, but felt trapped in that situation.

After the sale, I spent ten months investigating what I would do next and had narrowed my choices to three. I was having a terribly difficult time making my decision about which one to choose, which was odd for me. I'm usually good at making decisions, but I couldn't seem to make this one.

I needed to dig into what was keeping me from making that decision, then make it and move on with my life. At last, I decided to go on a personal retreat to get to the bottom of things. That is why I was on that beach that morning and why I hadn't spoken with anyone for six days.

And while walking along the beach I had an a-ha! moment. I suddenly identified what was keeping me from making the decision about what I would do next. It was an "I can't" message like that described in Chapter 11.

I uncovered an "I can't change my mind" story rattling around in my skull. In fact, it was "I can't change my mind about what I will do next, even if I later find I don't like the choice I've made." I had no idea where that notion came from and, really, its source made no difference.

I had felt trapped by the interminable sale process and was miserable. Combining that with my "I can't" story, my decision-blocking notion was this: "What if I choose poorly what I will do next and I am as unhappy as I was before? And worse yet, I can't change my mind?" That is what held my feet in concrete.

In that a-ha! moment, I saw that my assumption about not being able to change my mind was entirely untrue. I saw that if I chose poorly and later found I didn't like my choice, I could change my mind. I could stop doing what I had chosen, and pursue a different path instead.

A thousand pounds fell from my shoulders instantly. Just as fast, I was standing up straight and had a spring in my step. I decided what I would do next almost immediately. Indeed, it was easy, because, as explained in Chapter 11, once an "I can't" notion has been exposed, the issue becomes a simple "I will" or "I won't."

## DECIDED

After making that decision, I continued my walk. It was still early morning and people were starting to come out to the beach. I remember a young boy playing fetch with his golden retriever. An older gentleman and lady were placing chairs and an umbrella for their day on the beach. Farther down the beach, a woman was sitting with her back to the waves, facing the morning sun that was just coming over the roofs of the beach houses.

As I walked closer, I took in the scene in more and more detail. The woman was sitting on a camping chair, the kind that sits on the ground and has a seatback. She had one leg out straight and her other knee was up. She was wearing a wide-brimmed sunhat and sunglasses. I noticed she had one arm thrown casually over her shoulder and her long, blonde hair flowed over the seatback. And she looked absolutely lovely.

It occurred to me that it didn't do her any good if I only thought that—how lovely she looked—and kept it to myself. In that moment, I decided to obey an imperative I had learned on an adventure trip years before—to never let an opportunity to do or say something kind to slip by. Yes, I would tell her how lovely she looked.

Then the "I can't" story kicked in.

I couldn't tell her how lovely she looked, I told myself, because she'd think I was trying to pick her up. She would call me a jerk and tell me to get away from her. A full-blown rejection story clattered inside my skull in a nanosecond. Then I started arguing with myself as I told myself "Yes, I'll tell her," then "No, I can't do that." I was a nut case.

And I walked behind her—between her and the waves—so she didn't even see me. I went on for a few dozen more steps and at last stopped dead in my tracks and said to myself, "Jack, you big chicken!" I turned around and walked over to her, and we had that conversation. I remember it to this day as though it just happened.

"Excuse me," I said. She looked up and raised her sunglasses. I noticed how tanned she was and how her red nail polish contrasted with her skin.

"Yes," she said.

"I'm sorry to disturb you. You look so comfortable."

"No, that's all right. What is it?"

"Well, I saw you as I was walking down the beach, and I want to tell you how lovely you look sitting here just as you are."

She suddenly had a look of complete surprise. She paused for a moment, and said, "I can't believe it." Now I had the look of complete surprise. That wasn't at all a response I had expected.

"What do you mean?" I asked.

She said, "I'm about to turn forty, and I've been sitting here feeling old and unattractive. Now you come along and say that to me. You're my guardian angel!"

I was stunned. I knew nothing about her or her life circumstances or her self-image. I didn't know about her challenges, and I certainly had no expertise in the guardian angel business.

I did know I had come to the island to figure out why I was having difficulty making a decision about what I would do next and then make that decision. That was still true.

And in that moment I saw that I had also come to the island to get out from under the weight I had been carrying around so that I could show up fully—right here, right now—and simply tell the truth to that woman so she could hear what she needed to hear so that she could carry on.

When we do that—when we show up fully and tell the truth—only the finest things happen.

Consider this an invitation for you to be fully alive and on that field of play for the entire game of your life, so you can:

- Get more of what you want and less of what you don't want

- Live your fully empowered life—all of it.

- Make a positive difference in the lives of others.

And you will surely:

*Ignite A-Game Performance.*

# CHAPTER 15

# Action

*"One, two three, many."*

GEORGE GAMMOW
ONE, TWO, THREE ... INFINITY (MENTOR, 1947)

The Khoikhoi were an ancient and primitive tribe of people in southern Africa. Its people measured a man's wealth by how many head of Nguni cattle he owned. They were challenged, though, to differentiate among those with large herds because the numbering system of the Khoikhoi stopped at the number three. Everything after that was simply "many."

That speaks to the complexities human beings can handle comfortably. Perhaps you are familiar with the Rule of Three. We can remember three things. But when, for example, you offer to your direct reports a bullet point list of four items, upon your explaining the fourth one, they promptly forget number two and maybe number three as well. That is to say, too many items in a list will result in forgetting some. It may even lead to paralysis because there is simply too much to contemplate.

*Engagement* is all about action. So, now that you've read the Preface and the first 14 chapters, you've received a laundry list of practices on which to act, and perhaps you've made a list of things you intend to do.

So, because of this large number of suggested actions, there is an inherent risk of not acting at all. Let's make this actionable for you so you can start the process of positive change. After all, it is your actions that determine if you will get more of what you want and less of what you don't want.

On page 163 write a list of at least 3 actions you will take which will move you toward your "True North" (see Chapter 3). Then review your list and pick one action you will take within the next three days. You may not complete it immediately, but do get started.

Identify it and commit to it. Remember, that trip of one thousand miles truly does begin with your first step.

# Conclusion

*"The destination is irrelevant. It's about who you become along the way."*

MARK LEBLANC
AUTHOR OF *GROWING YOUR BUSINESS* AND
*NEVER BE THE SAME*

The Chicago neighborhood where I grew up was like family neighborhoods in most cities in the 1950s. The elementary school was across the street and just two blocks south was the commercial street with all the stores a family might need, all within walking distance. Tucked into the neighborhood was a branch of the Chicago Public Library, which we visited often. Before long, I was able to walk there myself, and each visit was a glorious experience.

Glorious and frustrating. There was so much to see and so much to read!

I was fascinated by the sheer number and variety of books. I wanted to read and enjoy all of them, yet I didn't know where to start. I simply wanted to experience *everything*. As a little kid, I had no words for that, but the feeling never left me.

Over time that desire—that wanting to experience everything—expanded to include all of life. I didn't have a fully conscious clarity about that until many years later.

I played sports with enormous joy. I went through school and met the wonderful woman who would become my wife. We had a girl and a boy. Along the way we acquired a golden retriever and a station wagon (what we had before SUVs and mini-vans) as well as a house with a huge yard and a big mortgage in a neighborhood full of kids. I started an industrial water treatment company and ran it for 25 years.

But something odd happened toward the end of that entrepreneurial time.

While I had achieved sufficient success, I had a lingering sensation that something wasn't quite right. It was like those exercises that ask, "What's missing from this picture?" and I had only a partial answer. I knew it had to do with giving back, and that led to a startling revelation.

## THE TEETER-TOTTER OF LIFE

Do you remember the playground at your elementary school or in your neighborhood park? Did you play on the teeter-totter, going up and down, up and down? I was always one of the biggest kids, which meant I could pretty well control the teeter-totter.

Take that image forward about forty-five years and imagine life as a teeter-totter. I had been blessed with an ability to make things happen, a reasonable tolerance for risk, and a strong work ethic well-learned from my parents.

I love succeeding, but I dislike failing even more, so I learned to do whatever it took to succeed on my terms. So far, on that teeter-totter of life, I'd had a pretty good ride.

But it turned out all that success was the problem and it pointed an arrow at the missing piece of the aforementioned picture.

I had received so much on one end of that teeter-totter that it needed to be rebalanced. To do that, I had to help make a difference for others, and I knew I had to find a way to do that quite directly.

## CEO FORUMS

A year after selling my company, I stumbled in a most serendipitous way onto TEC—The Executive Committee—now called Vistage International. Over the next ten years, I facilitated three TEC/Vistage groups as their chairman and we helped one another succeed according to how each individual defined success.

It was an everyday exhilaration to be with these people operating at the C-level. They were the polar opposite of the nefarious CEOs who make the headlines due to their unethical or illegal behavior. The folks in my groups—and in Vistage groups everywhere—aren't the "it's all about me" types. Indeed, often what concerned them most was the well-being of their employees. They were great people to be with and to coach.

Lucky me, I had a front row seat to see them in the human vulnerabilities of their CEO roles. I was blessed to be in a position to support them in monthly group meetings and in coaching sessions we called "1-2-1s" or "one-to-ones." My need to balance the teeter-totter of life was well-met by being in this place of service.

## A WALDEN MOMENT

Then one day an a-ha! moment arrived. What I felt as a child in that Chicago Public Library and all along the way was about wanting to experience all of the moment—to be fully present and live all of life. It was a "Walden moment." In the introduction to *Walden*, Henry David Thoreau wrote:

> *I went to the woods because I wished to live deliberately, to front only the essential facts of life, and see if I could not learn what it had to teach, and not, when I came to die, discover that I had not lived. I did not wish to live what was not life, living is so dear; nor did I wish to practice resignation, unless it was quite necessary. I wanted to live deep and suck out all the marrow of life, to live so*

*sturdily and Spartan-like as to put to rout all
that was not life...*[45]

That is what has always been so very important
to me. Thoreau's words defined a passion I had
always felt and could not name until then. And
this formed a connection to my CEOs, their
challenges and their opportunities.

## PRESENCE DRIVES SUCCESS

By that time, I had lived in the world of C-level
people both as a CEO and as a coach/observer,
and I had watched many struggle with their
leadership. The most effective leaders were those
able to bring out the best efforts from others.
And it was remarkable how clear it was that these
leaders showed up as fully present, being "right
here, right now" with those who looked to them
for leadership. That brought this clarity to me:
*Leadership presence* is a major piece of the core of
great leadership that drives success—the same
kind of presence I had always sensed all the way
back to my childhood and visiting the Chicago
Public Library.

Further, it has always been my belief that I had a
life job to do. In my a-ha! clarity about fully living
each moment of life, I saw my job as that of being
a wake-up call to others to fully live their lives,
to show up with their presence, and to create the
success they truly want.

That is what I intend the message in this book to deliver—a wake-up call to fully alive living and all it offers, and a construct to make that wake-up call actionable.

## A LIFELONG FOCUS ON PRESENCE

Since 2005, I have delivered hundreds of keynote presentations and workshops to leaders functioning at various levels of leadership in many organizations across the United States and Canada—businesses, associations and educational institutions. The constant theme of these programs is a focus on presence in the moment and how that influences others to be their best.

Taking this one step further, it isn't that only I have a specific job to do. I believe each of us has a life job to do—one that is unique to each individual.

Perhaps you hold that belief, too. Whatever your life job may be, your full presence will be required in order to do it well, with you as the CEO (Chief Engagement Officer) of your life. It will make all the difference in the results you achieve. It will determine the quality of your days and perhaps even the quantity of the years of your life.

It's common after my speeches or workshops for a few attendees to approach me to tell me how my message made a meaningful connection for them and how it spoke to their life circumstances. In those moments, they always teach me something important.

We are human beings first; everything else comes after that. And while being human encompasses a vast palette of attributes and capabilities, sounds and colors, feelings, thoughts and desires, a few basic things that we all share trump everything.

Most obvious, of course, is survival. One piece of survival requires us to please those who, in our infancy and early years, provided for our needs— those who ensured our survival. We looked to them for instruction, and we got a complex interconnectedness of guidance with the subtlest of cues. As we got older and more educated, our patterns of behavior and attitudes became far more sophisticated, but we remain human and our fundamental imperatives do not change.

All of this brings us back to the core issue of what we look for, what we desire, and what we need from our leaders. It is elegantly and exquisitely simple, because we need only three things, as described in Chapter 9:

## ENGAGEMENT

# THE CORE OF GREAT LEADERSHIP

Be *fully alive*, right here, right now

—

Demonstrate that you care

—

Validate: Let them know you believe in them

First, we human beings want our leaders to bring their presence, to be with us when they are with us, to be fully alive with us. In that focus, a meaningful connectedness is created that informs and inspires us. An individual's style is exactly that: *style*. It is the *substance* that matters to us, and we are profoundly positively affected when our leader shows up fully present with us.

Next, we need our leaders to care about us. As infants, we were concerned about our physical needs. We were also having our emotional needs met, such as the simple feeling of pleasure when Mom looked into our eyes or when anyone held us close.

As we grew, the caring took other forms such as someone listening to us, especially at times that were deeply important to us. Or it was the "atta boy" and "atta girl" offered by our leaders. We got the message clearly: They cared.

And there is one more part that is at the core of great leadership.

Life is uncertain and is, at times, enormously challenging. We may fear that our abilities are overmatched, that we are not up to the task. These are the times when we need those to whom we look for guidance to look us in the eye and let us know that they believe in us. They see something in us that affirms that we can succeed.

That simple belief emboldens us. As a result, we move ahead with a confidence and determination that is far more difficult to access without that validation. Indeed, knowing others believe in us can motivate us to achieve beyond any level we might have dreamed possible.

Those are the three core things leaders do that make them great leaders. When we as leaders engage at a level we had not engaged before, those who look to us for leadership begin to incrementally engage at a deeper level as well. And we all succeed beyond what we might have imagined.

If you are a leader, then by definition people follow you. They may want many things from you but they need very few. This book and my keynotes and workshops flesh out specific things you can do to encourage your people to give their best. And it all starts with you.

Again, it distills down to these three imperatives: Be fully alive with them, let them know that you care about them, and show that you believe in them.

Do these things and you will be well on your way to being a great leader, a *Chief Engagement Officer*. Then you and your people will be following this primary imperative:

## ENGAGEMENT Practice #10

# Live All of Your Life

# Gratitudes

My friend Gregg Levoy is the author of *Callings: Finding and Following an Authentic Life*. He has written a new book, *Vital Signs: The Nature and Nurture of Passion*, in which he wisely has a Gratitudes section, not an Acknowledgments section. I decided immediately that this issue really is far more about expressing gratitude than something as milquetoast as acknowledgements. Indeed, "acknowledgements" seems a bit like the parts listing for a lawnmower. So, my first mention is to Gregg for the label switch, as well as the idea to use matches on the cover. I have stolen both shamelessly, but with great gratitude.

I started down the leadership speaking path because I wanted to make a difference. I wanted to give back, to pay it forward for the boundless generosity of so many people who have helped me, for the great good fortune I've had, and even for the knocks on the head that have proven to be valuable lessons in disguise.

So, I thank first the countless wonderful leaders who have been unwitting teachers to me, who have shown themselves as the most human of beings in their role as leaders, and who have given so much of themselves.

I offer my thanks to the thousands of keynote and workshop attendees who have been so heartfelt in their praise, gratitude, and suggestions. Their feedback gives me the clarity and the jolt of energy to carry on full speed ahead.

My friends Rick Sack, Steve Wallman and I were on a boys long weekend in Scottsdale, AZ when I mentioned that I thought it was time to write this book. They skewered me by saying, "So, when will you do this?" Their encouragement got me to start, always the hardest part, so a big "thank you" goes to you, Rick and Steve.

I have coached dozens of C-level executives over the years, but, oddly, I never had a coach for myself until I began to write this book. I stumbled upon Marc LeBlanc in a most serendipitous way, just as I was first putting electronic pen to GUI paper. I learned he has been a successful businessman and professional speaker, that he is past president of the National Speakers Association, and—the best part—he is a published and successful author. Note that those two descriptors—published and successful—don't find their way into the same sentence for most writers. This is significant.

Even better, Mark coaches speakers and leaders of small businesses. His wisdom, insight, clarity, and insistence on execution are a large part of the reason for this book coming to fruition, so thank you, Mark. And because of what he has taught me, here is my last offer to you for how you can be the best leader you can be: If you don't have a coach, get one.

My editor, Barbara McNichol, dropped out of the sky and into this project with as much serendipity as that of my coach and, again, at exactly the right moment. She was referred to me by dear friends who probably did not realize that her skills at editing were applied so regularly to business related manuscripts. She was and is the kind of person I needed. That she corrects my stumbling grammar, punctuation, sentence structure, and chaotic flow of concepts with the lightest of touch makes her a delight to work with. I am grateful for her support.

As I came close to completing the manuscript for this book it became clear that some things might not be offered as clearly as they should be. That is to say, I could not avoid writing this book with some assumptions and understandings that a reader might not have, thereby delivering confusion instead of providing value. Because this is my work I was largely blind to such things, so I enlisted the help of my daughter Amy. She is a superb editor with a photographic memory of grammar and punctuation rules and an amazing facility for details. And, because she did not know the nuts and bolts of Engagement, she was an ideal person to proofread the manuscript with fresh eyes. I made every change she recommended. She's that good. Thank you so much, Sweetie.

Be clear, though, that if there are grammar, punctuation or flow-of-thought errors in this book, all responsibility for such stumblings are mine.

And I needed still more help. My son Scott is a most successful business executive and business developer and has the best social skills of anyone I know. Even with his jammed schedule he reviewed this book and offered important insights and specific suggestions for improvement, all of which I included. If you are a leader in business and this book speaks to you, say thanks to Scott. I'm saying thanks to him right now.

My parents, Dick and Muriel Altschuler, were my role models for clear articulation and a strong work ethic. They taught me the basics of human relationships, many of which are focused into this work and onto the role of leader. They were and remain my primary teachers of so much of life and I will ever be grateful to them for being the best they could be for me.

All of that is true, and without intending to dismiss so many who have given so much to me, my full-throated, flag-waving acknowledgment goes to my wife Marilyn. She is crazy enough to believe in me at times when there might not be much in evidence that doing so is a good idea. She tells me in a thousand ways she supports me, even when that leaves her alone so often because of my travels. She shares in my joys as well as my fears and is always the best barometer in evaluating my new creations.

Did I mention that she believes in me? That is one of the finest things truly great leaders do and I am her ever-devoted follower.

Thank you, beautiful Marilyn.

# Appendix

## EVERYTHING STARTS FROM YOUR "TRUE NORTH"

### Practice #1: Manage Things – Lead People

Manage things, like policies and procedures. But people become dispirited if they are micro-managed and find it nearly impossible to give their best. Instead, offer your greatest leadership.

### Practice #2: Ask Great Questions

To get the best from the people who look to you for leadership, you need to draw out their wisdom, their genius and their creativity. That won't happen if you supply all the answers and solutions. So, rather than giving your great answers, ask great questions. And abandon blaming. It just isn't useful.

### Practice #3: Listen

Show your respect by simply seeking to understand. People will feel cared for and will want to give more of their discretionary effort. Remember that,

*"Being listened to is so close to being loved
that most people cannot tell the difference."*
David Oxberg

### Practice #4: Deal With Conflict

There is no safety in playing it safe.
Avoiding conflict nearly always makes
things more difficult to deal with. To make
conflict conversations more productive,
positive and easier, follow the Fully Alive
Leadership Rules for Safe Conflict (Safe
= discharges the conflict and preserves the
relationship):

1. Abandon winning the argument

2. Listen – creates safety in the
   conversation

3. Stay focused on the goal

### Practice #5: Be Here Now

You're always here; the time is always
now. Nothing happens anywhere else. It
is where your most effective leadership
lives and breathes and it is where, when
and how you influence others to give their
A-game.

### Practice #6 Set the Bar High

People who look to you for leadership will
live up to or down to your expectations, so
set the bar high—not for you, but *because
they are too important to be anything less than
their best.*

## Practice #7: Deal With Reality

Not a story about reality that you may be telling yourself. Surface your "I Can't" beliefs so that you are no longer limited by them and instead have choices. Then you'll shift to "I will" or "I won't." You will always know what is best.

## Practice #8: Be Their Confident Captain

You don't have to have all the answers, nor be a Pollyanna. You simply need to demonstrate your confidence at all times that you and your team will succeed, that you believe in them.

## Practice #9: Commit

*Commit* is an absolute: You either do or you don't. There is no middle ground. It is binary. It is about being all-in. You have to choose to commit and it will make all the difference.

## Practice #10: Live All of Your Life

Get out of the stands and on to the field of play in the game of your life for the entire game.

## The Core of Great Leadership

- Be *fully* present—right here, right now

- Demonstrate that you care

- Validate—let them know you believe in them

# Disclaimer

Confidentiality and privacy are critically important things and I take them seriously. That is why, other than people and quotations identified in the body of this book or in the endnotes, the names of individuals detailed in these stories are pseudonyms. The events, however, are very real and occurred exactly as depicted.

# About The Author

Jack Altschuler has been a successful entrepreneur, trade association president and curious examiner of the ever-entertaining, often-baffling human condition. He has both observed and lived the challenges of leadership, enjoying the victories and rubbing the wounds. He hopes this book will help you to need to do less wound rubbing.

For ten years, Jack facilitated CEO roundtables under the auspices of The Executive Committee (TEC), now called Vistage International, Inc. He has delivered his message of leadership to thousands through his presentations focused on how leaders can influence others to give their best. In addition to his keynote presentations and workshops, he offers his ongoing contributions to leadership at:

http://www.FullyAliveLeadership.com.

Note: Most of his blogs can be read in less than thirty-nine seconds. No, really, thirty-nine seconds max. Subscription is free and your comments are encouraged for the betterment of all.

Jack and his wife live in Northbrook, Illinois, close to their children and grandchildren, where they share their house with a really big dog.

Share *Engagement* with your leaders, employees, colleagues, friends and family members. Email Jack at Jack@FullyAliveLeadership.com for special pricing on bulk quantities of twenty-five, fifty or more books.

# Endnotes

1. *The West Point Way of Leadership*, Col. Larry R. Donnithorne (Ret.), (Doubleday, New York, 2003) page 3.

2. "Dan Pink: The Puzzle of Motivation," July 2009 at TEDGlobal 2009, Oxford, England. http://www.ted.com/talks/dan_pink_on_motivation#t-793984.

3. *Drive: The Surprising Truth About What Motivates Us*, Daniel H. Pink (Riverhead Books, 2009) page 110.

4. "Does Leadership Really Make Any Difference?" by Richard Hadden and Bill Catlette. *Fresh Milk from Contented Cows* newsletter, August 2011. http://archive.constantcontact.com/fs024/1011313535112/archive/1107078149559.html.

5. *Drive: The Surprising Truth About What Motivates Us*, Daniel H. Pink, page 89.

6. "Driving Performance and Retention Through Employee Engagement, A Quantitative Analysis of Effective Engagement Strategies." Corporate Leadership Council of The Corporate Executive Board, 2005.

7.  "Employee Engagement: A Leading Indicator of Financial Performance." The Gallup Organization, 2011.

8.  "Increasing Employee Engagement by Fostering a Culture of RESPECT." Paul L. Marciano, Ph.D., President, Whiteboard, LLC, 2009.

9.  "Closing the Engagement Gap: A Road Map for Driving Superior Business Performance." Towers Perrin, 2008, page 18.

10. "The New Employment Deal: How Far, How Fast and How Enduring?" Towers Watson, 2010, page 18. Note: The Towers Perrin organization merged with the Watson Wyatt organization in 2009; hence the name change since the 2008 report referenced above.

11. While I have been speaking on the topic "True North" since 2005, Bill George has a wonderful exploration of this concept in his book *True North*, (Jassey-Bass Publishing, 2007).

12. Steve Isaf, CEO
    Interra International, Inc.
    Atlanta, GA

13. The official Toyota explanation of *The 5 Whys* can be found at: http://www.toyota-global.com/company/toyota_traditions/quality/mar_apr_2006.html.

Perhaps the best-known quality-related example of this exercise is in the realm of Six Sigma: http://www.isixsigma.com/tools-templates/cause-effect/determine-root-cause-5-whys/.

Another useful exploration may be found at http://blogs.hbr.org/2012/02/the-5-whys/.

14. While there has been much scholarly work examining human resistance to change, an accessible article on change by Lisa Quast can be found on the Forbes Magazine website at http://www.forbes.com/sites/lisaquast/2012/11/26/overcome-the-5-main-reasons-people-resist-change/.

Another clear piece is by Elizabeth Moss Kanter and can be found on the Harvard Business Review site at http://blogs.hbr.org/2012/09/ten-reasons-people-resist-change/.

15. *Future Shock*, Alvin Toffler, (Bantam Books, 1990) page 414.

Note: This book was originally published by Random House in 1970.

Alvin Toffler is reported to have said, *"The illiterate of the 21st century will not be those who cannot read and write, but those who cannot learn, unlearn, and relearn."* That statement is a more quotable form of one paragraph in *Future Shock*, which consists of both text written by Toffler and a quote from psychologist Herbert Gerjuoy. Scant evidence is available to indicate that Toffler ever uttered those exact words. Nevertheless, the point remains both valid and useful.

16. "Gen Y: Part II – Gen Y Opinions and Perspectives on Workplace Culture and Their Top Employers of Choice." CareerEdge Organization, 2011. Also, as reported in The Toronto Star, November 2, 2010: http://www. thestar.com/business/2010/11/02/study_ what_twentysomethings_want_from_their_ jobs.html.

17. Many thanks to Susan Scott of Fierce, Inc. and to Vistage International, Inc., the CEO roundtable organization, for this wonderful and most useful question.

18. "The Neuroscience of Leadership." David Rock and Jeffrey Schwartz, Strategy + Business, May 30, 2006. http://www.strategy-business.com/article/06207?pg=0.

19. *Fierce Conversations*, Susan Scott, Fierce Conversations, Inc., (Viking Penguin, New York, 2002).

20. *The Servant*, James C. Hunter, (Crown Business, New York, 1998), page 90.

21. *Hoosiers*, produced by Carter DeHaven and Angelo Pizzo, directed by David Anspaugh, Orion Pictures, 1986.

22. *The Seven Habits of Highly Effective People*, Stephen R. Covey, Franklin Covey Co., (Fireside Press, 2003).

23. "Iranian immigrant found guilty of murdering wife, relatives," Chicago Tribune, August 12, 2012 http://articles. chicagotribune.com/2012-08-24/news/ct-met-triple-murder-trial-0824-20120824_1_daryoush-ebrahimi-ileshvah-eyvazimooshabad-karolin-khooshabeh.

24. This quote has been attributed to David Oxberg, but the record is unclear. The source may have been Dr. David W. Augsberger, professor of Pastoral Care and Counseling at Fuller Theological Seminary. http://chuckwarnockblog.wordpress. com/2010/01/05/reveiw-pastoral-counseling-across-cultures-by-david-augsburger/.

25. "Respect," originally recorded by Otis Redding in 1965 and recorded by Aretha Franklin in 1967 on the Atlantic Records label. Words and music by Speedo Sims, updated by Otis Redding.

26. *The Heart of Conflict*, Brian Muldoon (G.P. Putnam's Sons, New York, NY 1996), page 30.

27. Ibid. page 63

28. Ibid. page 64

29. Ibid. page 199

30. Ibid. page 46

31. Ibid. page 30

32. "Are You Sure You're Not a Bad Boss?" by Jack Zenger and Joseph Folkman, Harvard Business Review blog, August 12, 2012. http://blogs.hbr.org/2012/08/are-you-sure-youre-not-a-bad-b/

For your convenience, you can download a single page list of the article's ten worst bad boss traits here: http://www.fullyaliveleadership.com/wp-content/uploads/2013/07/Bad-Boss.pdf.

33. An excellent nuts and bolts preparation model for a conflict conversation is offered on Pp. 148-158 of *Fierce Conversations* by Susan Scott.

34. *The Essential Rumi*, Jalal al-Din Rumi, translations by Coleman Barks, (HarperCollins, 1995) p. 36.

35. "Chicago Isn't Waiting for Superman." http://www.usnews.com/opinion/articles/2014/09/05/chicago-public-schools-show-real-graduation-rate-progress.

36. http://www.urbanprep.org/about/newsroom/news/100-percent-urban-prep-academy-seniors-going-college.

37. "Urban Prep Charter Academy for Young Men" aired on April 12, 2010 as a segment

on Chicago Tonight. Jay Shefsky, producer.
Find it here: http://chicagotonight.wttw.
com/2010/04/12/urban-prep-academy-
young-men.

38. http://www.urbanprep.org/about/creed.

39. *It's Your Ship: Management Techniques from
the Best Damn Ship in the Navy*, D. Michael
Abrashoff, Captain, (Hatchett Book Group,
rev. 2012).

40. Ibid. page 55

41. *Captain Phillips,* (Sony Pictures/Columbia
Pictures) 2013.

42. *Out of The Crisis*, W. Edwards Deming, (The
Massachusetts Institute of Technology,
Center for Advanced Educational Services,
Cambridge, MA, 1991) Pp 59-62.

43. Gene Kranz actually did not utter the famous
imperative during the Apollo 13 crisis, but
he embodied that message in his leadership.
Nevertheless, the sentence has been in
common use for decades and is part of urban
lore. It is portrayed in the movie *Apollo 13*
(Universal Pictures, 1995).

44. "Last Lecture: Achieving Your Childhood
Dreams." Randy Pausch, https://www.
youtube.com/watch?v=ji5_MqicxSo.

45. *Walden and Civil Disobedience*, Henry David
Thoreau, introduced by Michael Meyer,

(Penguin Books USA, Inc., New York) p. 135.
Note: this book was originally called *Walden;
or, Life in the Woods* and was first published
in the United States in 1854 by Ticknor and
Fields.

# NOTES

# ACTIONS I COMMIT* TO TAKE SO THAT I GET MORE OF WHAT I WANT AND LESS OF WHAT I DON'T WANT

_____

_____

_____

_____

_____

_____

_____

_____

_____

_____

_____

_____

_____

_____

_____

*See Chapter 13

Made in the USA
Middletown, DE
30 June 2015